West Virginia's COVERED BRIDGES
A Pictorial Heritage

Drawing by
BILL WINTZ

Technical Consultant
Dr. Emory L. Kemp

By Stan Cohen

Color Photos by
Steve Shaluta Jr.

Pictorial Histories Publishing Co., Inc.
Charleston, West Virginia

COPYRIGHT © 1992 STAN B. COHEN

All rights reserved. No part of this book
may be used or reproduced without written
permission of the publisher.

LIBRARY OF CONGRESS
CATALOG CARD NUMBER 92-80003

ISBN 0-929521-55-2

First Printing   April 1992

Typography by Leslie R. Maricelli
Cover Art by Linda J.C. Turner
Cover Design by Mike Egeler

Printed in U.S.A.

PICTORIAL HISTORIES PUBLISHING CO., INC.
4103 Virginia Avenue Southeast
Charleston, West Virginia 25304

Preface

Covered bridges hold a fascination for many people around the country. They are a reminder of the past—a more gentle time—and they are an engineering marvel in this day of high technology.

There were more than 10,000 covered bridges built across the United States between 1805, when the first was erected in Philadelphia, and the early 1900s. As of 1992 only 893 of these remain, with three-quarters of them found in six states—221 in Pennsylvania, 157 in Ohio, 103 in Indiana, 100 in Vermont, 54 in Oregon and 52 in New Hampshire.

Throughout the entire nineteenth century, the covered bridge was an essential part of the transportation system in West Virginia. The total number of bridges constructed is unknown, but there must have been hundreds. There were still more than 54 in existence in the early 1950s, but by 1979 the number had been reduced to 19. In 1992 17 remain, some in good condition, some in need of repair or restoration.

All 17 extant covered bridges in West Virginia were listed on the National Register of Historic Places as a theme group in 1981 following research and preparation by Dr. Emory L. Kemp of Morgantown.

I became acquainted with the state's covered bridges years ago while doing research on West Virginia's historic sites. Much of the state's history has been lost through the years as a result of disinterest, neglect and lack of funding. But with the increased interest of local and state governments and concerned citizens, the fate of this one segment of our state's history will, I hope, be secure for future generations.

The almost complete destruction of West Virginia's premier covered bridge at Philippi in 1989 brought the plight of all the state's covered bridges to the attention of officials and historians. The total reconstruction of this bridge in 1991, giving it back its original 1852 look, is not only a tribute to the dedicated government authorities and citizens who made it possible, but also a tribute to the men who did the work, much as the craftsmen did in 1852.

Dr. Kemp has been the leader in raising people's awareness of the plight of the remaining covered bridges, and stands as a "knight in shining armor" for preserving them, or, to use a more poignant term, as the saviour of the bridges. For many years he worked, along with others, to promote the idea of bridge protection and restoration, and with his recently established Institute for the History of Technology and Industrial Archaeology in Morgantown, the fate of the remaining 17 bridges is in good hands.

This book is mainly a pictorial record of each of the remaining covered bridges, with an expanded description of the history, destruction and rebirth of the Philippi bridge, surely one of the greatest wooden bridge restoration projects in the United States. In addition, I have included descriptions of many of the bridges that are long gone.

I also have given a brief history of the road system in the state, as this was the reason for building these bridges, and have included a short primer on bridge types to give the reader some background information.

Much of the material for this book was gleaned from Eva Margaret Carnes' book, *Centennial History of the Philippi Covered Bridge, 1852-1952*, published by the Barbour County Historical Society; Myrtle Auvil's fine book, *Covered Bridges of West Virginia, Past and Present*, published by McClain Printing Company; the pamphlet, *Covered Bridges in West Virginia*, produced by Barbara Howe and Dr. Emory L. Kemp for the Publication and Printing Services at West Virginia University under a partial grant from the Humanities Foundation of West Virginia. It is part of a slide/tape show which can be lent to interested parties upon written request; and lastly, the files of the Historic Preservation Unit of the West Virginia Department of Culture and History.

This book could not have been completed without the assistance of Dr. Emory L. Kemp and Paul and David Marshall of Paul Marshall & Associates of Charleston, Mike Pauley and Rodney Collins of the Historic Preservation Unit, Steve Shaluta Jr. of Charleston and Linda J.C. Turner of Jane Lew.

My thanks also to Gordon Blair Lee of the restoration team on the Philippi Bridge, Bill McNeel of Marlinton, Don Rice of Elkins, Bill Wintz of St. Albans, Tim McKinney of Fayette County, Billy Joe Peyton of the Institute for the History of Technology and Industrial Archaeology in Morgantown, Margaret Conner of Charleston and the staff of the West Virginia State Archives, the West Virginia & Regional History Collection at West Virginia University, Greenbrier County Historical Society and Jacquelyn McGiffert, who edited this manuscript.

Stan Cohen

Photo Sources

HPU — Historic Preservation Unit
WVU — West Virginia & Regional History Collection
SWV — State of West Virginia Archives

Why Were The Bridges Covered?

There is a controversy as to why bridges were built with a roof and sides. Was it done to protect and preserve the wooden span or perhaps to provide shelter for travelers during inclement weather?

Another explanation was offered by a man from Illinois: "Bridges were covered in the horse-and-buggy days because some horses feared crossing over water. With the bridge covered, the horses got the impression they were entering a barn, and they went right across."

But a man in Pennsylvania countered: "They would only have had to build a wall seven feet high on each side so they couldn't see the water."

Someone else suggested that covered bridges were built in northern states to keep ice off the floor, as horses would not cross an icy bridge.

Or we could choose to think that bridges were covered to provide shade for fishermen who could hang poles out the side vents or to serve as a refuge for courting couples looking for a little privacy.

The best explanation, however, is that the cover protected the underlying bridge timbers, which were assembled of green timber and left unpainted, from rain and snow, freezing and thawing. Moisture could not get into the joints of the bridge and rot them. Replacing or reshingling a roof was a simple matter compared to replacing members of the span.

At any rate, the world is a little nicer and more interesting with the presence of those covered bridges that are still in existence.

Contents

Introduction 6
The Turnpike System 6
Bridge Technology 7
End of an Era 7
Typical Wooden Truss Systems 8
Lemuel Chenoweth, the Bridge Builder 9

Section I
The Seventeen Remaining Covered Bridges in West Virginia

Barrackville	16	Laurel Creek	48
Carrollton	22	Locust Creek	50
Center Point	26	Mud River	52
Dents Run	30	Philippi	56
Fish Creek	34	Sarvis Fork	70
Fletcher	36	Simpson Creek	74
Herns Mill	38	Staats Mill	76
Hokes Mill	42	Walkersville	82
Indian Creek	44		

Section II
Bridges Gone and Forgotten in W.Va. 85
About the Author 107
About the Artist 107
About the Cover Painting and Limited Edition Print 107
About the Photographer 108

Introduction*

Covered bridges and turnpikes were an integral part of the early transportation system in West Virginia. The covered bridge, now a picturesque reminder of the past, was an essential component of the turnpike system that evolved in western Virginia prior to the Civil War. The network of turnpikes throughout the region influenced both the strategies and tactics of the Union and Confederate armies that occupied western Virginia as troops battled for control of roads and bridges.

The Turnpike System

Turnpikes originated in England during the seventeenth century, and the technology and engineering techniques used in building them were transplanted to America in the early nineteenth century. The covered bridge, however, was a central European invention, native to the area that is now Germany, Switzerland and Austria. Gradually European technology for the construction of turnpikes and covered bridges was adopted in America, and the closely related technological designs of each contributed to the other's success. By the early nineteenth century, Virginia's increasing population, urbanization and westward expansion necessitated a statewide transportation system to create new markets and increase western trade. In 1816 the Virginia Board of Public Works was formed to oversee and fund various "internal improvement" projects, as transportation systems were called then. Turnpike companies used both public and private funds to construct roads and bridges.

In western Virginia, however, the construction of turnpikes lagged far behind that of the eastern counties. Mountains and deep river valleys formed natural impediments to road construction, and the expense of overcoming these obstacles

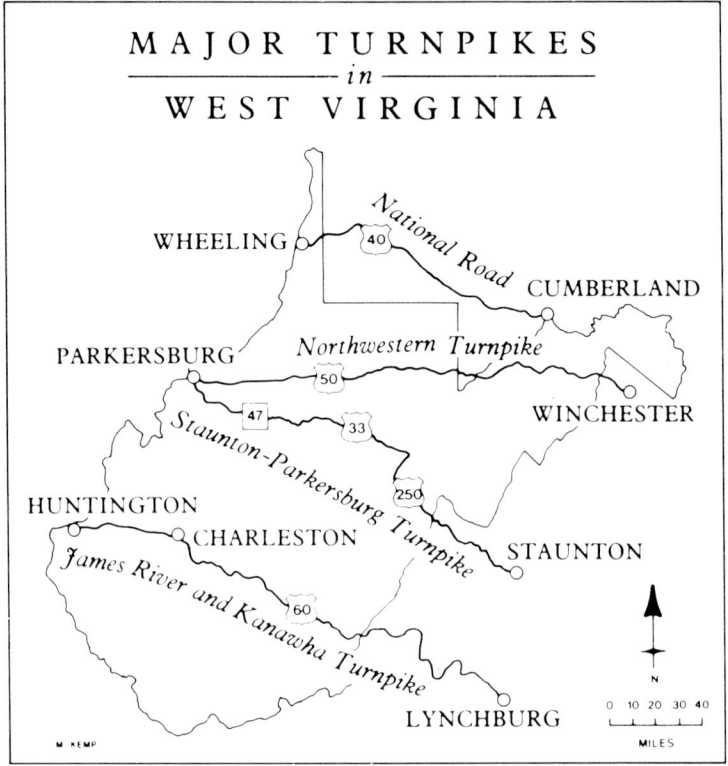

Cartography by Mark A. Kemp

was often prohibitive. Moreover, matching funds were more readily obtained in the more populated eastern areas. In addition, many leading legislators in eastern Virginia were wealthy farmers and merchants who gained economic advantages by concentrating improvements in the east. The limited number of "internal improvements" in western Virginia contributed to sectional differences between the two regions. The ensuing dispute was one reason for the separation and formation of West Virginia, a new state, independent of Virginia.

Bridge Technology

The early covered bridges located along the turnpike system in western Virginia were constructed entirely of wood. Large trees were felled to produce the necessary hand-hewn timbers.

The most important aspect of the covered bridge is the truss system. The truss is an arrangement of rigid triangles composed of small timbers which can be combined to form a strong and stiff structure. Because the members are held together with pins, they carry the loads efficiently in direct tension (stretching) or compression (pushing together.) In West Virginia seven basic truss designs were used: the Long, Howe, Warren, Kingpost, Queenpost, Multiple Kingpost and Multiple Kingpost with Burr Arch. In many cases, such as that of the Philippi covered bridge in Barbour County, the designs were modified to meet local needs.

Contracts for the construction of turnpikes and associated covered bridges were based on competitive bidding. Bids were let and contracts awarded to craftsmen who could provide a sound structure at a reasonable cost.

End of an Era

Several factors contributed to the demise of the turnpike system: the advent of the railroad, the continuous expense required for maintenance of the system, and the limited amount of public funds available.

With an expanding network of railroads, another type of bridge had to be found to support the enormous weight of locomotives. Iron was the answer. It provided the necessary strength and was non-combustible. (Fire had been a constant danger plaguing the wooden covered bridges.) Furthermore, since iron was weather-resistant, the roof and siding that had been required for the protection of the wooden truss was no longer necessary.

Iron permitted the construction of pre-fabricated bridges that could be ordered quickly and economically, in contrast to handcrafted covered bridges, and thus the craftsman's role diminished. Following the Civil War, the engineer attained prominence in bridge construction, and what had earlier been considered an art became a science, based on engineering principles.

The state gradually abandoned the turnpike system but did not set up a State Department of Public Roads until 1909. Several of the turnpike routes in West Virginia were improved and incorporated into the state's highway system, most notably U.S. 60, which follows the James River and Kanawha Turnpike; U.S. 50, which follows the Northwestern Turnpike; and U.S. 40, which follows the National Road.

For many small towns in West Virginia, the covered bridge remained an inexpensive solution for spanning little creeks and rivers. It is the small, rurally located, covered bridge that evokes in people today a sense of nostalgia for the romantic past.

A number of these covered bridges in West Virginia remain in use and provide access to remote areas of the state, but they are a rapidly disappearing symbol of the state's history. Time and the elements continue to exact their toll on these historic structures. The floods that devastated much of the state in November 1985 damaged a number of them.

In 1947 there were 89 covered bridges still standing in the state, but in 1992 only 17 remain. Thus in a 45-year period 72 bridges, or more than 1 1/2 per year, were lost. At this rate, nearly all of West Virginia's covered bridges will have disappeared by the year 2000.

*Information from the brochure, *Covered Bridges in West Virginia*, partially funded by the Humanities Foundation of West Virginia. Script by: Glenn V. Longacre, Dr. Barbara J. Howe, Dr. Emory L. Kemp and Jeffrey Harpold.

Typical Wooden Truss Systems *

Howe

The Howe Truss was introduced into bridge construction in the 1840s. The vertical rods were constructed of metal. The Mud River bridge, located in Cabell County, is the only existing example of a Howe Truss covered bridge in West Virginia.

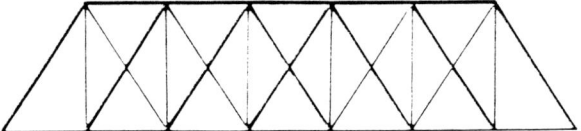

Long

The Long Truss was named for its designer, Stephen Long, a graduate of Dartmouth College and an instructor of engineering at West Point. Long's design was very popular and was used by several builders. The Long Truss allowed spans to reach 100 feet. In West Virginia there are six covered bridges that employ the Long Truss or a modified version of it. They are: the Philippi Bridge in Barbour County, Hokes Mill Bridge in Greenbrier County, Sarvis Fork and Staats Mill bridges in Jackson County, Center Point Bridge in Doddridge County and Indian Creek Bridge in Monroe County.

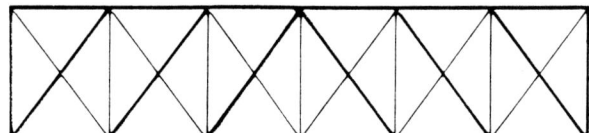

Warren (Double)

The Warren Truss was patented by two Englishmen, James Warren and T.W. Morzani, in 1838. The Locust Creek Bridge in Pocahontas County is the sole example in West Virginia of one variation, a Warren Double Intersection Truss. This bridge is also one of the few remaining timber Warren Trusses standing today.

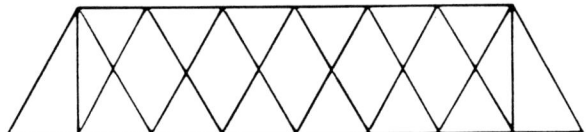

Kingpost

The Kingpost Truss is one of the oldest and simplest truss designs. Its origins can be traced to the Middle Ages, and it was one of the first designs to be used in building covered bridges in West Virginia. The Kingpost Truss allows spans to reach up to 40 feet. West Virginia contains two examples of this truss: the Dents Run Bridge in Monongalia County and the Fish Creek Bridge in Wetzel County.

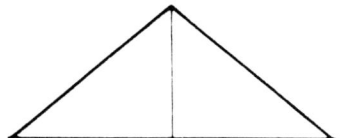

Multiple Kingpost

The multiple Kingpost was a Kingpost Truss modified by adding more triangles to the truss design. The design allowed spans to reach 80 feet. There are two covered bridges in West Virginia built with this design: the Fletcher and Simpson Creek bridges in Harrison County.

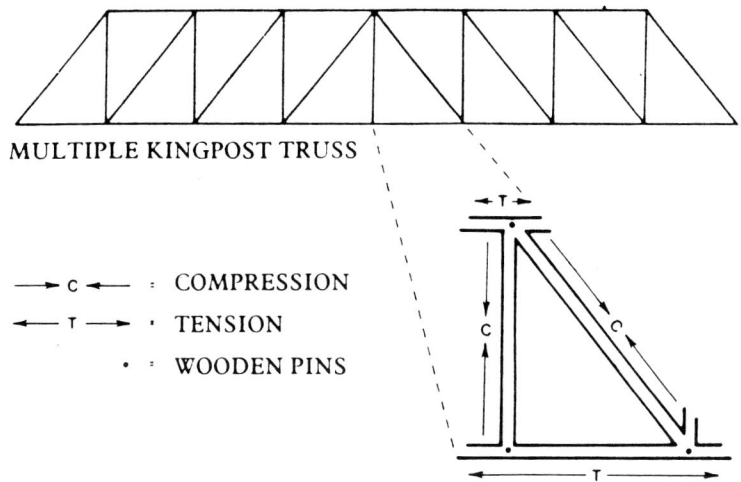

MULTIPLE KINGPOST TRUSS

— C — : COMPRESSION
— T — : TENSION
• • : WOODEN PINS

*Truss drawings by Mark A. Kemp

Queenpost

The Queenpost Truss, a version of the Kingpost, was modified by the addition of a horizontal cross-supporting member, which allowed for spans to reach 60 feet. Three covered bridges in West Virginia use the Queenpost Truss. They are: the Walkersville Bridge in Lewis County, Laurel Creek Bridge in Monroe County, and Herns Mill Bridge in Greenbrier County.

Burr Arch

The Burr Arch was designed by Theodore Burr, of Torringford, Conn., and patented in 1817. It featured a large wooden arch added to a conventional Multiple Kingpost Truss to increase the stiffness of the bridge. The ends were embedded in the abutments on both sides of the bridge and greatly increased the strength of the bridge as well as its stiffness. This system made it possible for covered bridges to be built as long as 350 feet without immediate supports. West Virginia contains two examples of the Burr Arch Truss: the Barrackville Bridge in Marion County and the Carrollton Bridge in Barbour County. The Philippi Bridge design is similar to the Burr Truss, but its truss is the Long rather than the Multiple Kingpost.

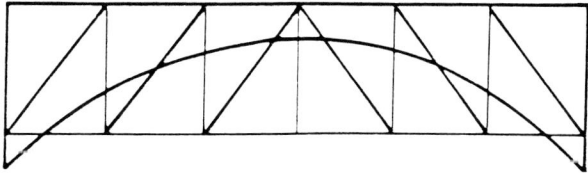

Lemuel Chenoweth, the Bridge Builder

Lemuel Chenoweth, a grandson of John and Mary Pugh Chenoweth, who settled in Randolph County in the late 1700s, was born on June 25, 1811 in Beverly, Randolph County, Virginia (now West Virginia). He was one of eight children of John I. and Mary Skidmore Chenoweth.

On June 23, 1836 he married Nancy Ann Hart, the great-granddaughter of John Hart, a signer of the Declaration of Independence, and the daughter of John Hart, whose farm on Rich Mountain was the site of a Civil War battle on July 11, 1861.

Chenoweth had a great interest in designing and building with wood, and he pursued studies to advance this interest at every opportunity, while at the same time providing for a family of 13 children. He is credited with the construction of covered bridges, churches and houses as well as buggies, wagons, sideboards, poster beds, a model of a reverse-cutting sawmill and even dominoes. There is evidence that he was experimenting with an invention of machinery for laying the Atlantic Cable. The present-day Huttonsville Presbyterian Church in Randolph County was built by him in 1883, and the old Beverly jail was built in 1891.

Although his formal education was meager, he attended the "pauper" schools of his time and also was tutored. He has been described as having an unusual aptitude for mathematics and is said to have mastered higher mathematics, including calculus, in three months. He attributed his propensity for learning to his parents' encouragement and his devotion to the Bible.

He was a proponent of the development of the region which was supported by the construction of the Staunton and Parkersburg Turnpike in the 1840s. He held county and state offices and served as county commissioner in 1841, a trustee of the Beverly Community in 1848, county coroner in 1855 and a member of the West Virginia state legislature in 1871.

Chenoweth's greatest recognition came from building covered bridges in western Virginia. His many bridges included the Beverly Bridge (1847), the Philippi Bridge (1852) and the Barrackville Bridge (1853).

A unique design for covered bridges has traditionally been attributed to Chenoweth, but the basic structural design of his bridges evolved from the Burr Arch Truss principle. Chenoweth learned to incorporate some of his own features into the Burr design, and what really led to his recognition as the prime bridge-builder was the structural integrity provided by his craftsmanship and the cost factor.

Lemuel Chenoweth and his wife, Nancy Ann Hart Chenoweth, taken from the original daguerreotypes. DON RICE

There are variations of a story based on an incident that happened in 1850 when he was bidding in Richmond for the construction of bridges in western Virginia. He is reported to have demonstrated the strength of his design by suspending the model of a covered bridge between two chairs and standing on it. He had, by this time, already built some small covered bridges and a large one at Beverly.

Chenoweth died at his home in Beverly on Aug. 26, 1887, and his wife, Nancy, died in Beverly on May 8, 1912. They are both buried in the Beverly cemetery. Of their 13 children, 10 lived to be adults. Joseph Hart, the second oldest, joined the Confederate Army and was killed in action in 1862. Lou Ella May, the 10th child, lived until 1939.

Artifacts that belonged to the Chenoweth family. Lemuel's model sawmill is on the table in the middle. The model is now on display in the Randolph County Historical Society Museum in Beverly. It is a working scale model of a two-way, up and down sash sawmill. It is designated as "two-way" because the saw cuts as the carriage goes in each direction and as "up and down" because it cuts on both the up and down strokes. The actual mill would have been powered by water, and although the design appears primitive, it represents the first improvement over the whip saw, one which was simply pulled through a log by two men.

This house, built by Lemuel Chenoweth in 1847, is now privately owned. It is located just southeast of the old Beverly bridge site on the route to Rich Mountain.

Three old gentlemen pose in front of the Beverly Bridge, date unknown. The sign over the entrance states: "$5 fine for running or driving over this bridge faster than a walk." MRS. MARGARET CONNER

This bridge, no longer standing, was built by Lemuel Chenoweth in 1847 to span the Tygart River at Beverly, on the Staunton and Parkersburg Turnpike. Seen here in a photo taken in the 1920s, the bridge was partially destroyed by Confederate General Rosser's forces in 1865 but was rebuilt by Chenoweth in 1873. The state dismantled the bridge in 1951 and erected the present one. DON RICE

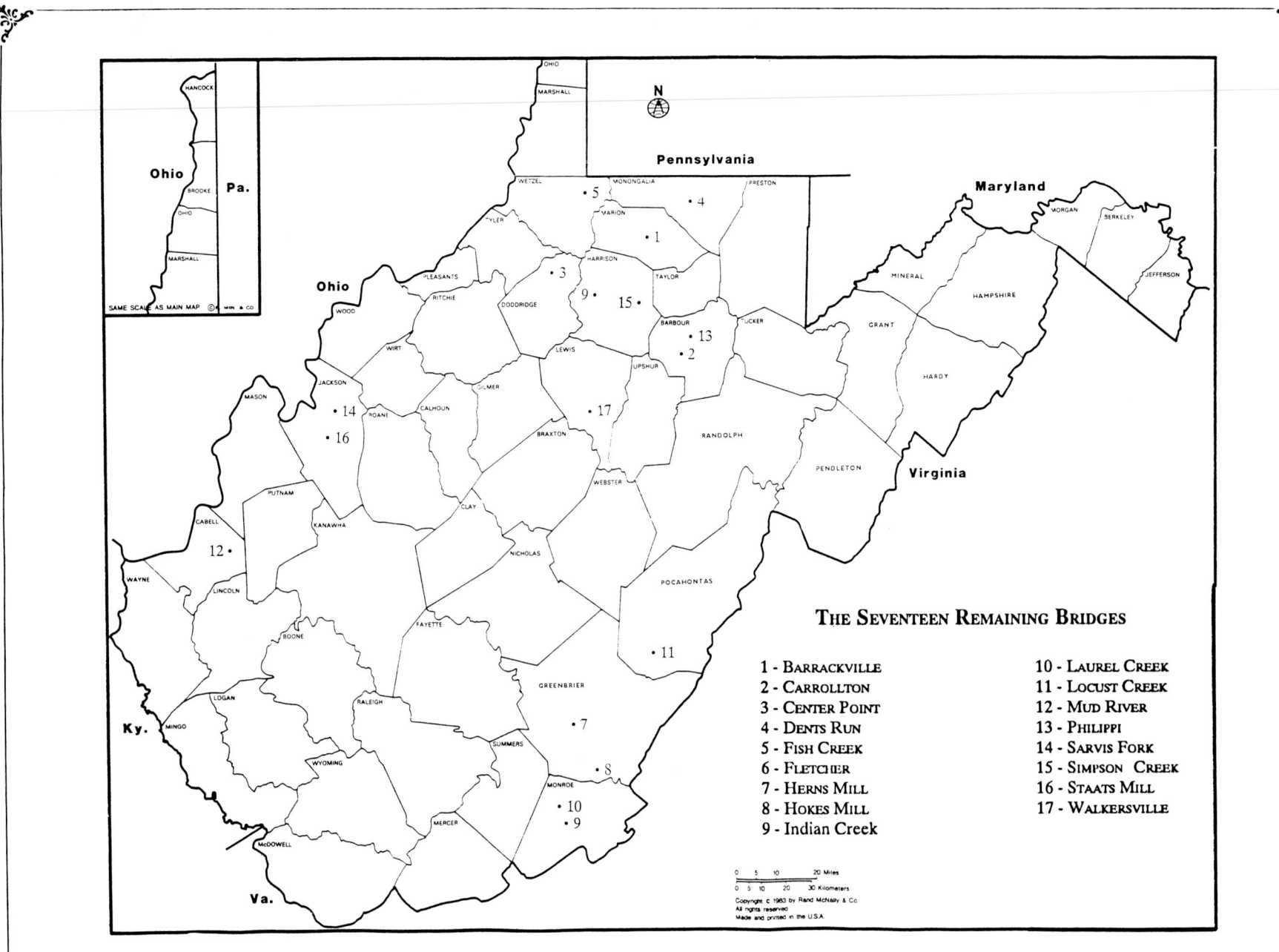

Section 1

The Seventeen Remaining Bridges in West Virginia

Barrackville Bridge

MARION COUNTY

Location: Across Buffalo Creek on County Route 250/32 at Barrackville, west of Fairmont.
Truss type: Multiple Kingpost with Burr Arch.
Length: 145' 9-3/4"
Width: 20'

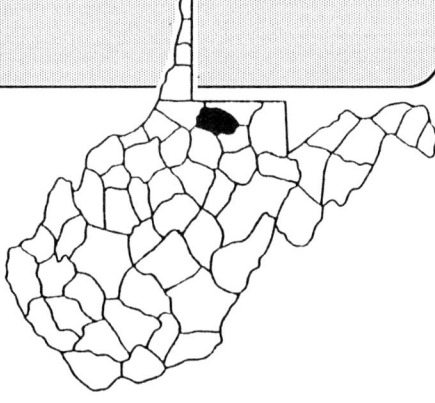

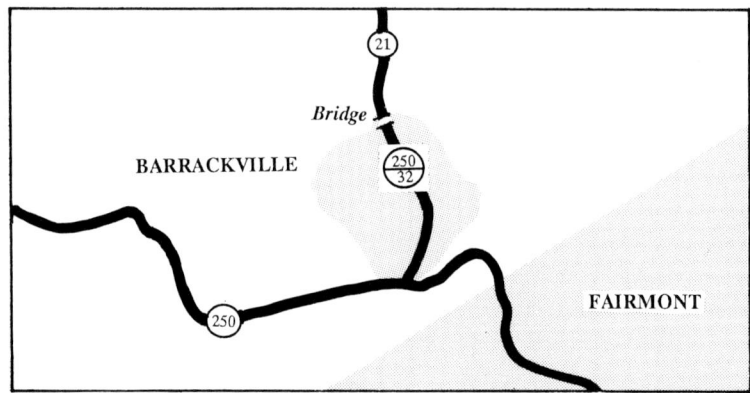

Lemuel Chenoweth is considered the premier builder of covered bridges in West Virginia. Of the many that he built, two are still standing. One is the bridge at Philippi, his greatest accomplishment, which has recently been restored. The second is the bridge across Buffalo Creek at Barrackville in Marion County.

This bridge, built in 1853, is the second oldest and at 145 feet, 9-3\4 inches, the longest clear span in the state, and is a further tribute to the bridge-building capabilities of Chenoweth and his brother, Eli. It stands as an excellent example of a modified Burr Truss, and its construction took fewer than five months, which is not so remarkable considering that the Chenoweth brothers had built about 10 similar bridges in the preceding 10 years. A sidewalk was added in 1934 and the siding and roof are of a later vintage but the main structural framework seems to be original in every aspect.

It is located near the 18th Century site of Ice's Mill, and was saved from destruction by the family, who were Confederate sympathizers and who convinced the army to spare it during Gen. William E. Jones' raid through the area.

The bridge was built on the Fairmont-Wheeling Turnpike, a feeder road of the Staunton and Parkersburg Turnpike. The Fairmont-Wheeling Turnpike was financed mainly by the State of Virginia. Originally conceived as a way of developing, on a commercial basis, the newly settled area north of the Staunton and Parkersburg Turnpike and south of the Northwestern Turnpike, the road was extended to Wheeling when that city took on new importance in the 1850s.

At least part of the intention of the promoters of the project was to provide a route to compete with the Northwestern Turnpike, the National Road and the newly opened Baltimore and Ohio Railroad, all of which served to enrich Baltimore and Philadelphia, at the expense of Richmond.

The contract, signed by Superintendent Austin Merrill on April 25, 1853, required the Chenoweths to post a performance bond of $3,500. The contract was approved in Richmond on

Early 1900s view of the Barrackville Bridge across Buffalo Creek. WVU

July 6, and construction began shortly afterward. The cost of the superstructure was $12.50 per lineal foot, and since its length was 145 feet, 9-3/4 inches, it is assumed that the final cost was about $1,822. The bridge was built without siding or side walk.

The main framing consists of two multiple Kingpost trusses, each flanked by a pair of arches. This is a typical Burr Truss system, with 16 vertical posts. The panels at center span and the panels at either end have cross diagonal bracing (a variation of the typical Burr Truss design, which consists of diagonals inclined toward the center), while the remaining panels have only one diagonal.

The floor is supported by the lower chord of the truss. The road surface of 2" x 4" timbers is laid on edge perpendicular to the flow of traffic and supported by 11" x 3" stringers, laid face down. The stringers are then carried by both the secondary transverse members (3" x 12" x 19') spaced at one-foot intervals, and the main transverse members (8" x 15" x 19') on 10 foot, two inch centers.

The roof truss is made up of a series of transverse members reaching from the vertical posts of one truss to the other. Between each of these transverse members is cross-bracing of

4"x 6" pieces secured by "treenails" (wooden pegs) and wedges.

The foundation for the bridge consists of a north and south abutment built from stone cut into squares of approximately three feet and fitted together without mortar. The transverse members directly over the ends of the arch are supported additionally with 9-1\4" x 9-1\4" vertical timbers. Four vertical posts of the truss are connected to the arch ends, which in turn are located on concrete pedestals poured on the abutment (a modification of the original supports).

Horizontal shiplap sheathing was added about 20 years later to protect the bridge from the elements. In 1934 the present sidewalk was added, the approaches improved, steel rod hangers added to the truss from the arch to the bottom chord, and the bridge was painted. In 1951 supports were added to the floor stringers.

In 1987, a Bailey bridge was placed next to the bridge to carry traffic, and in 1991 the State Highway Department added more support to the floor and closed the bridge to vehicular traffic. A new bridge will be built to carry traffic across Buffalo Creek, and the old covered bridge will eventually be restored to its original 1850's appearance.

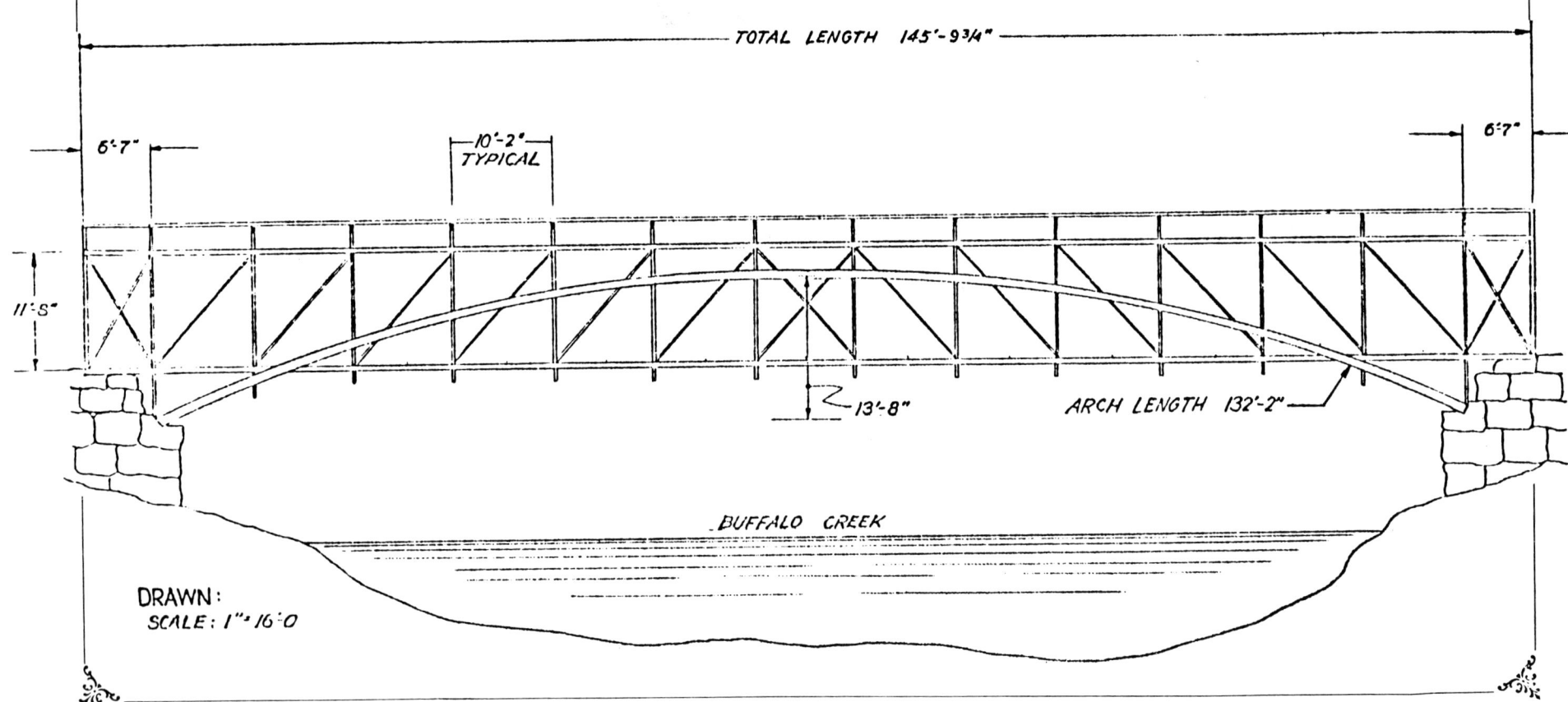

THE BARRACKVILLE BRIDGE ARCH TRUSS   Illustration by Richard Smith

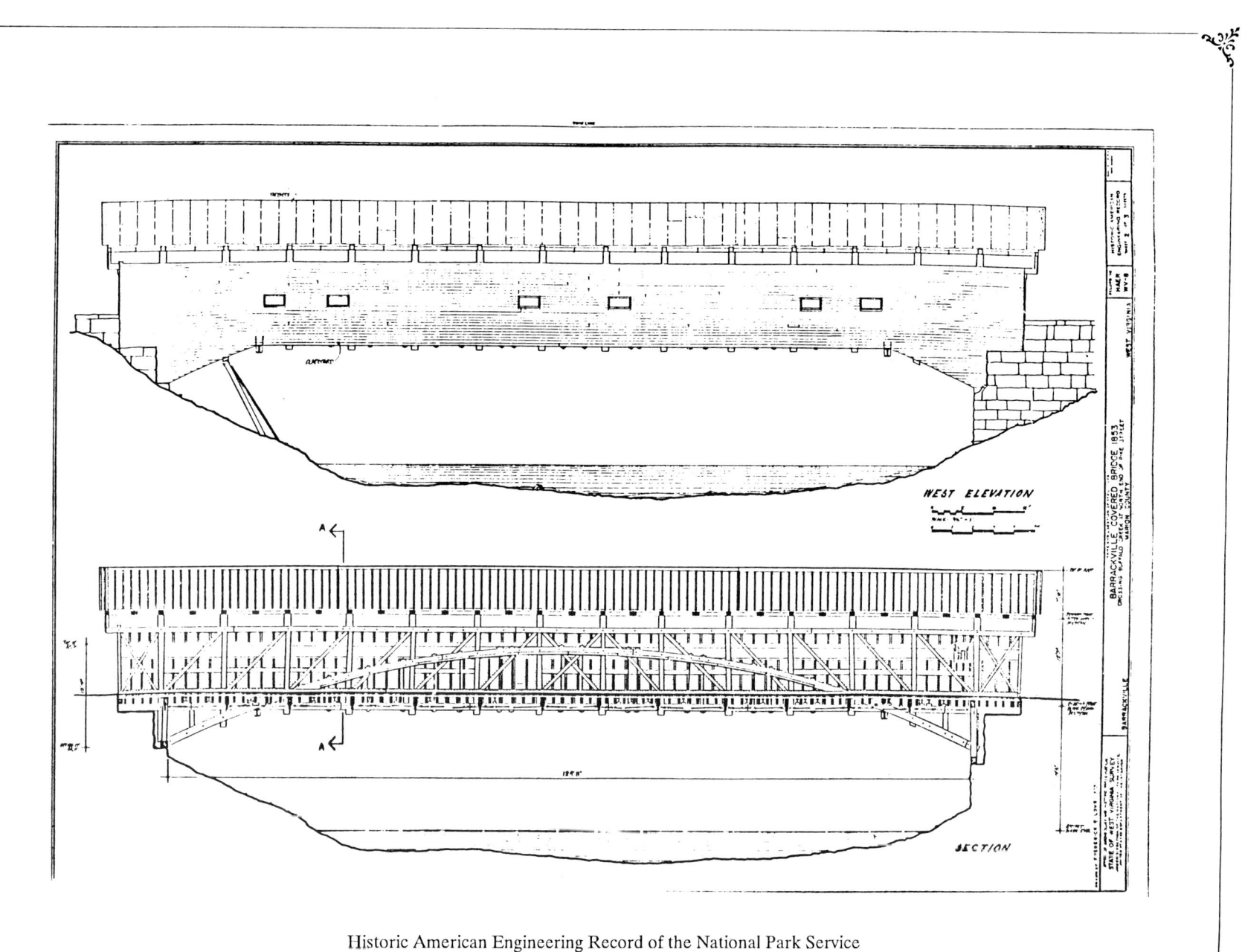

Historic American Engineering Record of the National Park Service

BARRACKVILLE BRIDGE 1983
HPU

BARRACKVILLE BRIDGE

Carrollton Bridge

BARBOUR COUNTY

Location: On County Route 36 across the Buckhannon River at Carrollton.
Truss type: Multiple Kingpost with Burr Arch
Length: 140' 9"
Width: 16'

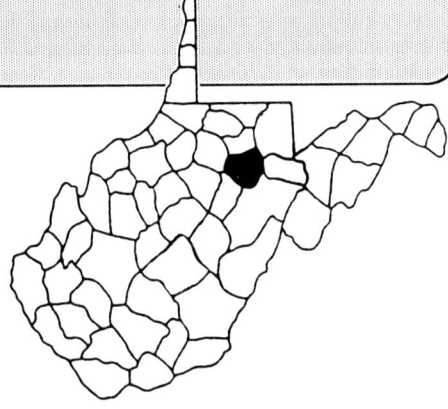

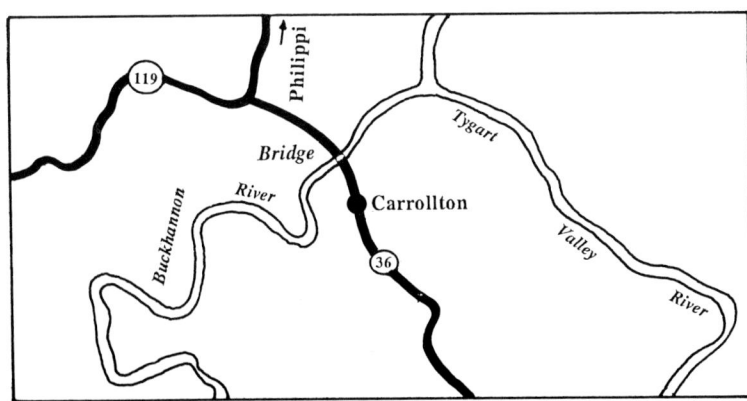

The Carrollton Bridge, one of two remaining covered bridges in Barbour County, is the second longest clear span and third oldest in the state. It is one of three which was built using the Burr Arch system.

Emmett and Daniel O'Brien, contractors for the bridge, which crosses the Buckhannon River on the old Middle Fork Turnpike, raised the superstructure in November, 1855. Construction was completed the following fall. Emmett, a native of Beverly, W. Va., had been the masonry contractor for the more famous covered bridge at Philippi.

The Carrollton Bridge superstructure is an excellent example of the patented Burr Arch type, and consists of two multiple Kingpost trusses, with panels 10 feet, one inch long and 11 feet, three inches high, each sandwiched between a two-piece arch made up of 7 1/2" x 15" timbers. The ends of the 7" x 9" diagonals fit into the enlarged, inclined ends of the 7" x 12" verticals. The bottom chords are composed of two 7" x 12 3/4" members, and approximately seven feet below the bottom chords, the ends of the arches rest on the abutments. The distance from the center line of the arch to the bottom of the two 7" x 8 1/2" members making up the top chord is three feet. Noteworthy features of the trusses are the massive center posts, which are tapered to a minimum width of eight inches and flare out at the top to a maximum width of 18 inches.

The original cost of the bridge was $2,928 for the abutments and $1,891 for the superstructure.

In 1962 the bridge was judged to be unsafe, but local community efforts saved it from destruction and brought about a subsequent renovation the following year. The timber deck was replaced by concrete consisting of a 150-foot three-span deck with a 12-foot roadway and a three-foot sidewalk supported by steel girders with two additionals piers in the river. In 1978 an additional $78,000 was spent on reroofing and on repairs to the bridge's wooden bracing and siding. Additional repair for damage inflicted on the truss work by a coal truck will be completed in 1992.

Carrollton Bridge. MIKE KELLER

Carrollton Bridge. SWV

CARROLLTON BRIDGE

Center Point Bridge
DODDRIDGE COUNTY

Location: On State Route 23 just south of Center Point, 12 miles north of U.S. 50. Crosses Pike Fork of McElory Creek.
Truss Type: Long
Length: 42' 1"
Width: 12' 6"

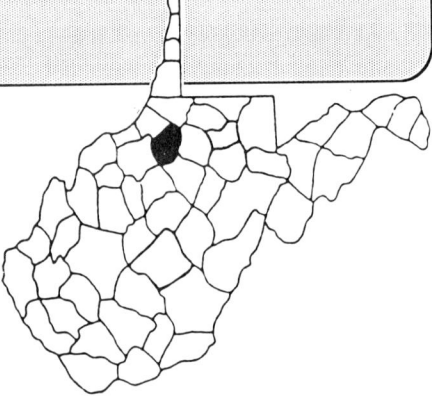

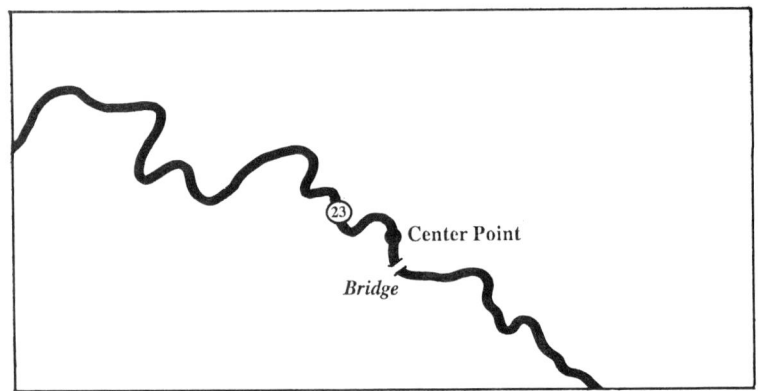

On July 13, 1888, the Doddridge County Court ordered that G.W. Ice be appointed a commissioner to supply specifications for a bridge to span the Middle Fork of the McElroy Creek in the McClellan District. Ice was also ordered to advertise and let out the contract for building the bridge and to supervise its construction. The records indicate that T.W. Ancell and E. Underwood built the abutments and John Ash and S.H. Smith the superstructures for at least two bridges in the McClennan District.

The Center Point Bridge is the only remaining covered bridge in Doddridge County. It is 12.6 feet wide and 42.1 feet long, with board-and-batten siding and a sheet metal roof.

The trusses are of the patented Long type, with four panels, each 12 feet high and an average of 10 feet, four inches long. Each panel has two 4"x8" diagonals angled toward the centerpost and a 4" x 6" diagonal fitted between and pinned to the double diagonals, sloping away from the centerpost. The diagonals fit flush against the top and bottom chord, which consists of two 4" x 8" and two 5" x 11 1/2" members. The single diagonals protrude

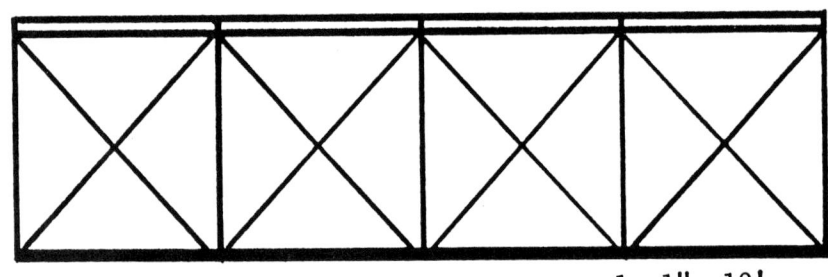

scale 1"= 10'   floor level

A Long system of four "X" panels. Each "X" is made up of three timbers bolted together at the center of the "X".

through and are pinned to the top and bottom chord.

A pipe, 7 1/2 inches in diameter, is the only structural reinforcement or alteration which can be seen. It has be secured to the underside of the downstream lower chord to help reinforce it.

The bridge was in regular use until 1940, when it became privately owned. Then in 1981 the owners donated it to the Doddridge County Historical Society, and citizens of the small community of Center Point donated their time to restore the bridge as a community project.

The Center Point Bridge as it looked in 1979-80, before restoration by the citizens of the community. HPU

Interior details of the Center Point Bridge in 1976. HPU

Center Point Bridge

Dents Run Bridge
MONONGALIA COUNTY

Location: On County Route 43/4, .7 mile off of County Route 43, off of U.S. 19 south of Westover. Crosses Dents Run.
Truss type: Kingpost
Length: 40'
Width: 12' 10"

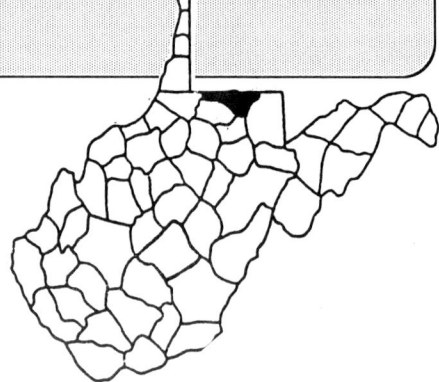

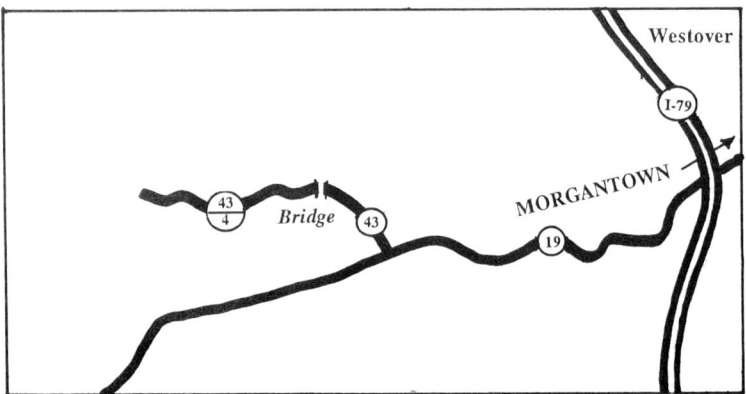

The Dents Run Bridge is one of only two examples in West Virginia of Kingpost Truss construction. It was built in response to a March 5, 1889, petition from Martin P. Fox and others to the Monongalia County Court. W. Y. Loar built the abutments, and William and Joseph Mercer built the superstructure.

The 40-foot structure has a Kingpost Truss. The floor is crosswise with two lengthwise runners. The bridge is supported by cut stone abutments without mortar. Structural steel has been added to the underside of the bridge for additional support. The bridge is covered with a tin roof and red-lap siding. Still open for traffic, the bridge is not used because of an adjacent concrete bridge.

The north side, west end view of Dents Run Bridge in 1981. HPU

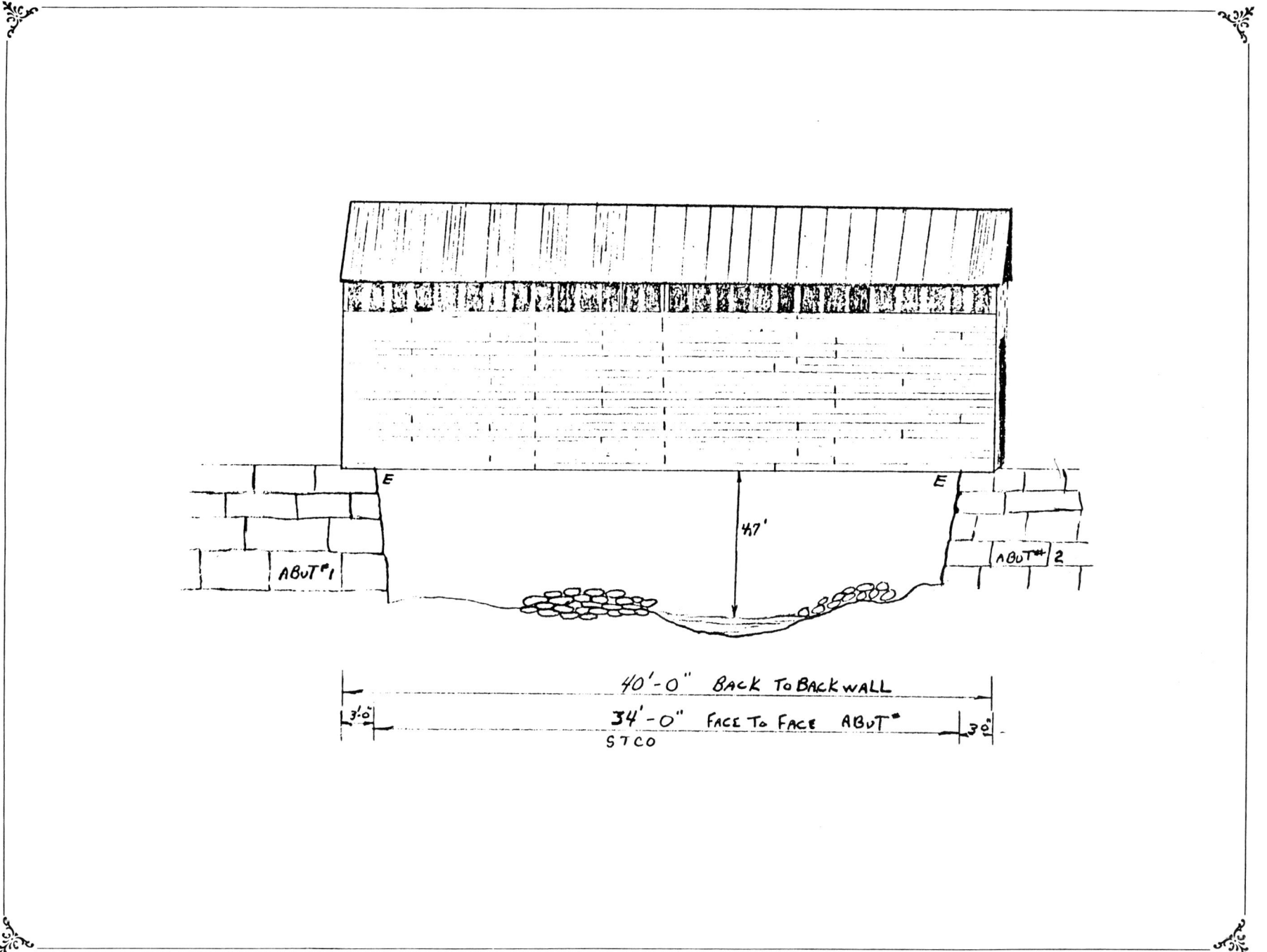

Two scenes of the restoration and rebuilding of the bridge in 1984.
HPU

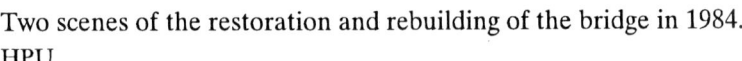

Dents Run Bridge

Fish Creek Bridge
WETZEL COUNTY

Location: On County Route 13 off U.S. 250 east of Hundred.
Truss type: Kingpost
Length: 36'
Width: 12' 10"

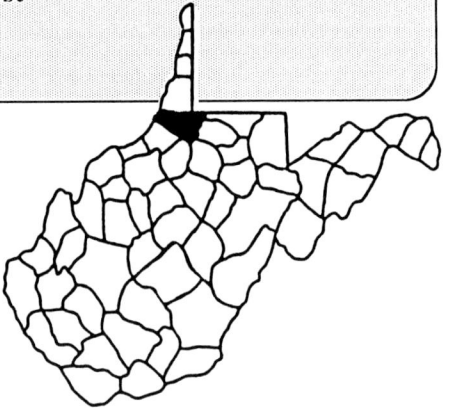

Few details of the history of the Fish Creek Bridge in Wetzel County are known. It is located near Hundred, the county seat, and is thought to have been built in 1880 or 1881 by relatives of C.W. Critchfield. The bridge is 36 feet long and 12 feet, 10 inches wide. It is still in use and is in fair condition.

Interior and exterior views of the Fish Creek Bridge on County Route 13. HPU

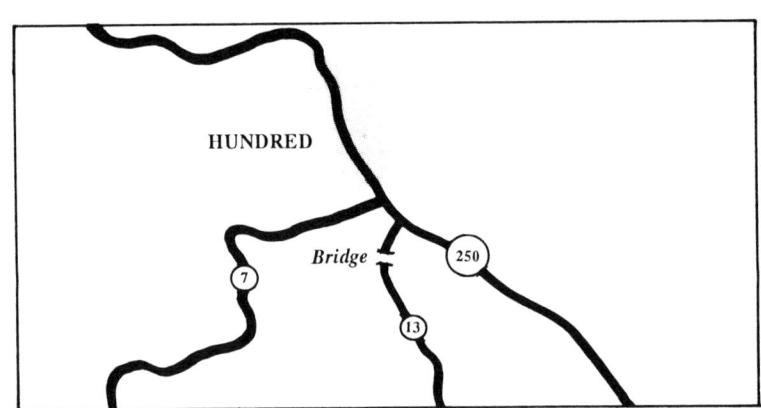

Fish Creek Bridge

Fletcher Bridge
HARRISON COUNTY

Location: On County Route 5/29, .6 miles off of County Route 5, north of U.S. 50 and west of Wolf Summit. Crosses the righthand fork of Ten Mile Creek.
Truss type: Multiple Kingpost
Length: 58' 4"
Width: 12' 4"

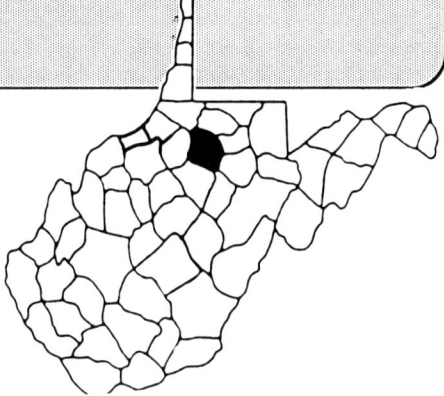

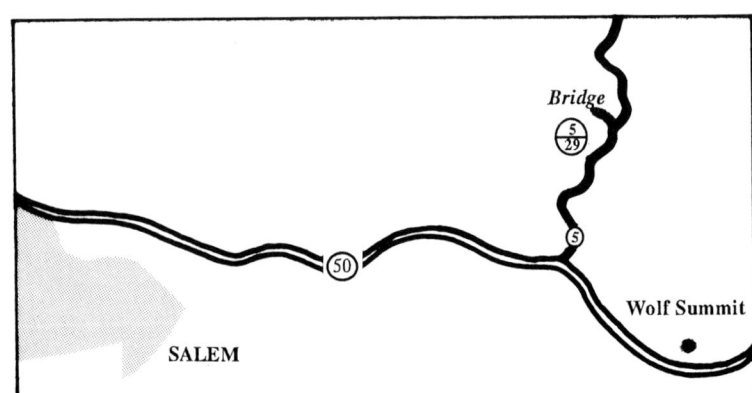

On July 1, 1891, the Harrison County Court authorized County Commissioner John T. Williams to advertise for bids for building a covered bridge across Tenmile Creek near the community of Marshville.

William J. Williams was appointed construction superintendent, and L.E. Sturm was awarded the contract for masonry construction. The superstructure was built using a Kingpost Truss system, and stones for the abutments were quarried at the top of a hill near the bridge site. The total building cost was $1,372.

One of only two remaining bridges in Harrison County, the Fletcher Bridge has not been significantly altered since it was built and is still in use, although it is in need of repair.

Entrance to the Fletcher Bridge. HPU

Fletcher Bridge

Herns Mill Bridge
GREENBRIER COUNTY

Location: On County Route 40, 2.2 miles south of U.S. 60, 2.6 miles west of Lewisburg. Crosses Milligans Creek.
Truss type: Queenpost
Length: 53' 8"
Width: 10' 6"

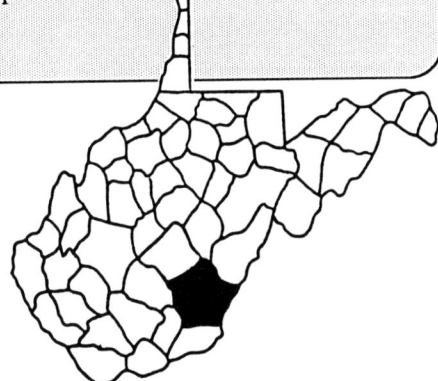

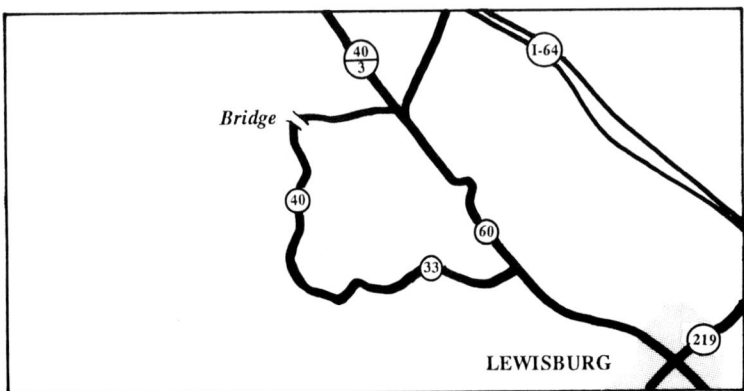

The Herns Mill Bridge spans Milligan Creek near Center Point in Greenbrier County. It was built for about $800 in accordance with an 1884 order of the Greenbrier County Court. The bridge was built with a Queenpost Truss design, but the names of the builders have been lost. At one time the bridge provided access to the S.S. Herns Mill. It is one of two remaining covered bridges in the county.

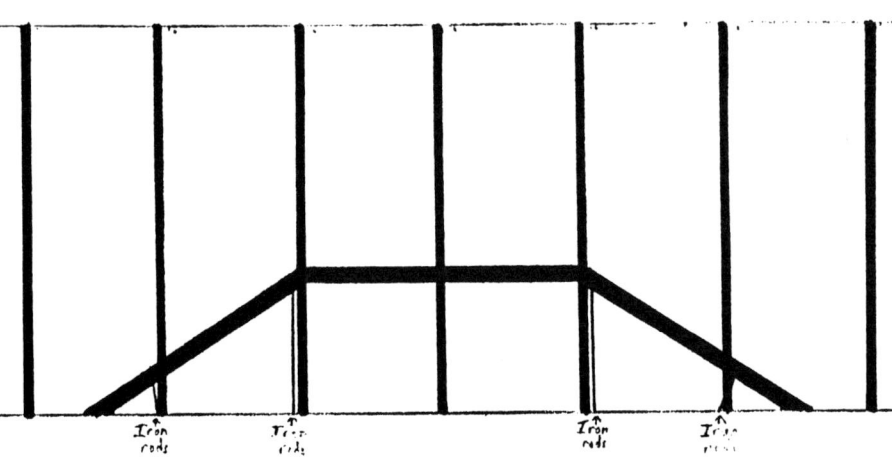

A central Queenpost with additional vertical supports and iron rods.

Photo by Gerald Ratliff

Interior and exterior views of the Herns Mill Bridge. There is a question as to whether the bridge was built in 1879 or 1884. HPU

Herns Mill Bridge

Hokes Mill Bridge

GREENBRIER COUNTY

Location: On County Route 62 off County Route 48, off U.S. 219 south from Ronceverte. Crosses Second Creek.
Truss type: Long
Length: 81' 6"
Width: 12'

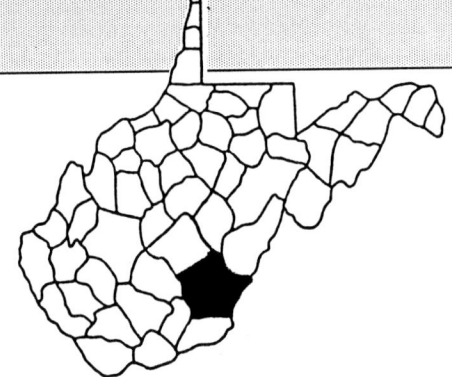

One of two remaining covered bridges in Greenbrier County, the Hokes Mill Bridge is still in use but is in only fair condition. During the July 1886 term, the county court authorized that $100 from the county treasury and $100 from the road fund be spent to build a bridge over Second Creek at what was known as Hokes Mill. It was built in 1897-99 using a modified Long Truss.

Interior and exterior views of the Hokes Mill Bridge. HPU

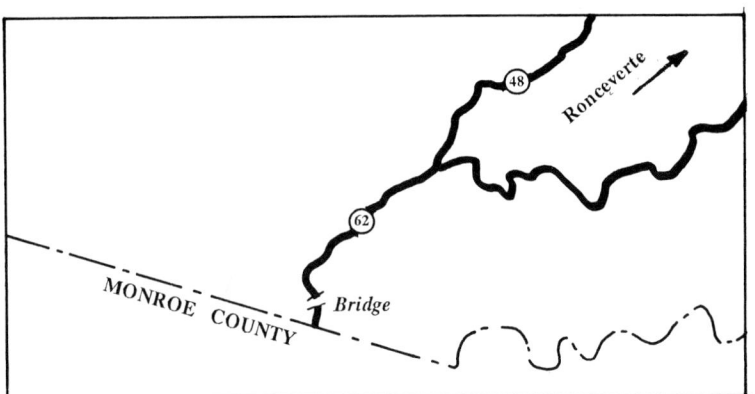

Hokes Mill Bridge

Indian Creek Bridge

MONROE COUNTY

Location: On U.S. 219 across Indian Creek, 3 miles south of Salt Sulphur Springs and 6 miles south of Union.
Truss type: Long
Length: 49' 3"
Width: 11' 7-1/2"

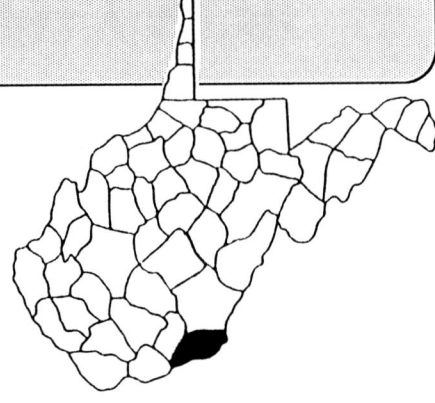

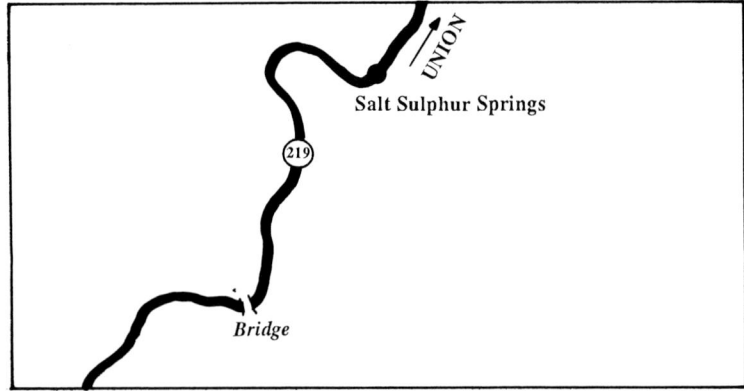

Indian Creek Bridge is both a tribute to the industriousness and ingenuity of its two young builders and a landmark in the developing rural transportation system in the area of Monroe County.

The county, located in the extreme southeast of West Virginia, was quite rural and sparsely settled in the late nineteenth century. The natural barrier of Peters Mountain blocked much commerce to the east and south, and internal transportation was rudimentary except between the frequented springs resorts. Off the "beaten path" of main roads, railroads and waterways, what routes did exist were often narrow and dusty or muddy, and they faced natural barriers of terrain and water. These roads usually crossed the water at established fords.

As the twentieth century approached, the Monroe County Court took an increased interest in upgrading the road system, and it participated in funding several improvements. One such improvement was proposed for the Indian Creek area south of Union and Salt Sulphur Springs, and a contract for the construction of a covered bridge was awarded to Oscar and Ray Weikel in 1898.

The brothers were only 16 and 18 years old, and their guarantee for the bridge was backed by their uncles, who ran a sawmill in the county. The authorities at first wanted an arched structure, but the Weikels applied techniques acquired through self-education and common sense to design their own plans, and a level-floored bridge was agreed to.

The young men industriously undertook the task, setting up their own sawmill near the site and preparing all materials but the iron rods, nails and shingles. Logs were delivered to the sawmill by oxen, and the finished products were transported to the construction location by horse and wagon. Their ingenuity shows in the tool that they developed to lift large timbers into place. It was a sort of doubled-geared, back-action cant hook which was attached to each end of the timber and handled by as many as four men. The completed bridge was accepted by the county at a cost of about $400, and it was in continuous use for about 30 years. At present all four corners of the bridge are badly rotted and it is urgently in need of repair.

The Indian Creek Bridge established the Weikel brothers in the lumber business in Monroe and Greenbrier counties, and it also bolstered the transportation system of the area for at least 30 years. But in 1929 or 1930 U.S. Route 219 was opened through the southern portion of Monroe County, and the old covered bridge was no longer needed.

In 1965 the Monroe County Historical Society obtained a 20-year renewable lease on the bridge and a right-of-way from the bridge to the highway. Contributions were given for repairs to make the structure "safe, sound and lasting," but at the same time to keep its original appearance. Antique vehicles, of the kind that were used on the bridge, were placed in it in 1966. There's a one-horse sleigh, a single-horse buggy, a surrey with a top and a lightweight farm wagon.

Oscar Weikel, one of the builders, wrote from Santa Rosa, Calif., to the *Monroe Watchman* on Feb. 17, 1965:

"I am more than interested in the old bridge as I was one of the contractors that built the bridge, and the youngest contractors in Monroe County at that time.

"As one of our first contract jobs, my brother Ray Weikel, age 18, and I built the covered bridge. I was 16 years old at the time.

"About the shingles, they were split and shaved chestnut. The bridge was made of pine lumber, we sawed the timber on the hill above the Old Harvey Baker place. We manufactured all the timber on our own mill, we were the lowest bidders on the bridge and our Uncles E.P. Smith Brothers told the County Court that they would stand behind us and we were granted the contract.

"I am 81 years of age and the bridge is still standing close to my heart. It does my heart good to know there are so many people interested in restoring the old covered bridge..."

Interior views of the Indian Creek Bridge showing some of the antique vehicles owned by the Monroe County Historical Society. HPU

Photo by Gerald Ratliff

Indian Creek Bridge

Laurel Creek Bridge

MONROE COUNTY

Location: On County Route 219/11, off County Route 219/7, south of Salt Sulphur Springs at U.S. 219, south of Union. Crosses Laurel Creek.
Truss type: Queenpost
Length: 24' 5"
Width: 13' 2-1/2"

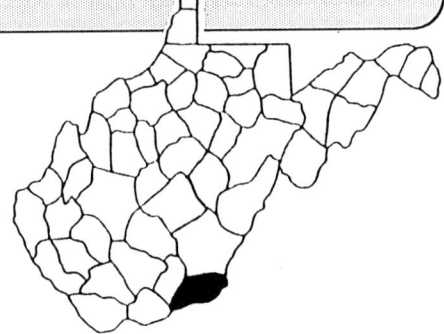

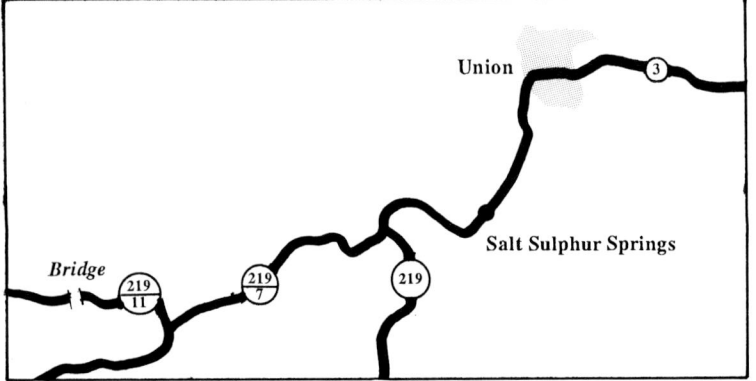

The smallest covered bridge in West Virginia is also one of the two remaining in Monroe County. It was built in 1910 or 1911 by Lewis Miller, who built the stone abutments, and Robert Arnott, who built the superstructure. The initial cost was $365.

The bridge is a little longer than 24 feet, and the simple structure contains no vertical bracing inside. The roof was originally covered with hand-hewn chestnut shakes.

Although it is still in use, the bridge is in only fair condition.

Interior view of the Laurel Creek Bridge, 1973. HPU

Laurel Creek Bridge

Locust Creek Bridge

POCAHONTAS COUNTY

Location: On County Route 31, 6.3 miles south of Hillsboro near the entrance to Calvin Price State Forest. Crosses Locust Creek.
Truss type: Warren Double Intersection
Length: 113' 9"
Width: 13' 6"

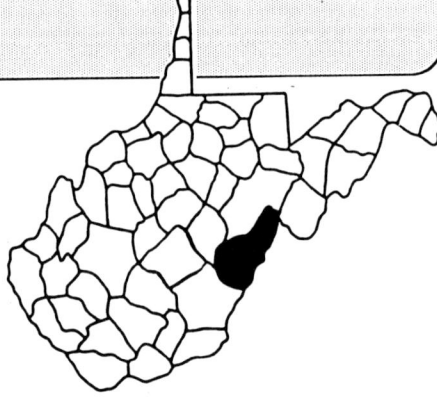

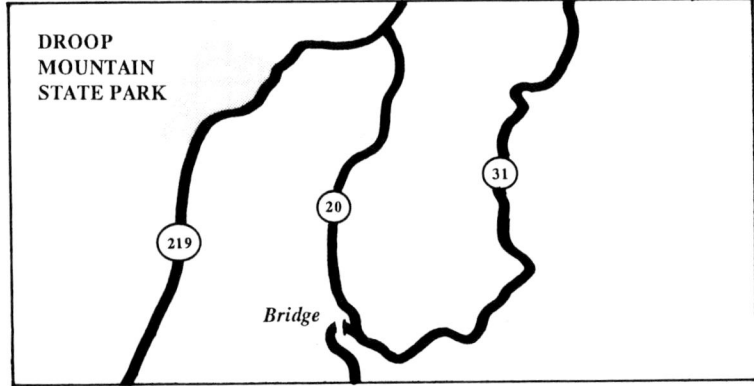

The last remaining covered bridge in Pocahontas County, constructed in 1888 on the original road established by pioneers linking Pocahontas and Greenbrier counties, crosses Locust Creek. The contractor was R.N. Bruce and the County Court paid him his contract price of $1,250 plus $75 for extra labor on the abutments.

Records indicate that a bridge was located on this site as early as 1822. The first bridge was constructed by Thomas Casebolt. This was probably the first bridge of any size within Pocahontas County. The need for a bridge at this location was compounded by the fact that Josiah Beard used the stream as a mill pond for his grist mill which would have made the water too deep for a ford. It is not clear if this first bridge was the one replaced in 1888 but it may well have been. In 1847 and 1868 the County Court ordered new bridges constructed but then had the old one repaired. It is not known if this bridge was a covered bridge.

By 1904 the present bridge was in disrepair due to a decaying roof. W.M. Irvine rebuilt the interior supports, trusses, sides and roof of the bridge as it is today. In 1990 a new bridge was constructed beside the covered bridge. Now owned by the state, the covered bridge is open to foot traffic only.

Bridge abutments, 1984. HPU

Locust Creek Bridge

Mud River Bridge
CABELL COUNTY

Location: On County Route 25 across Mud River, just south of U.S. 60 at Milton.
Truss Type: Howe
Length: 112'
Width: 14' 1"

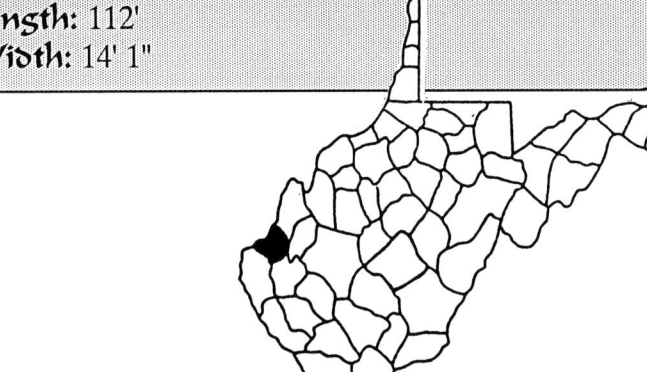

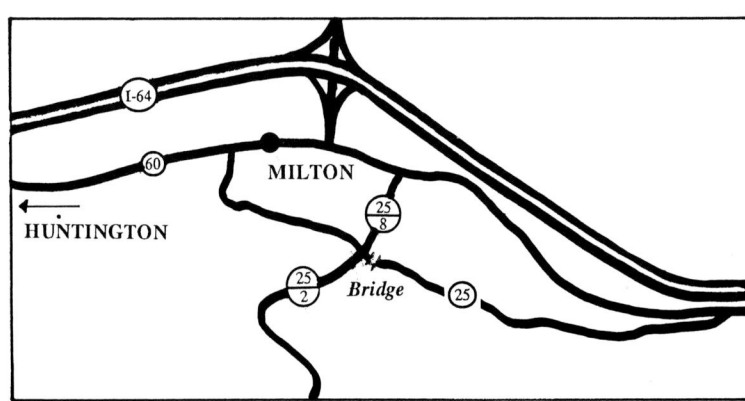

The original Mud River Bridge was built in 1834 and replaced in 1955 with a concrete deck and steel girder bridge. It had been a focal point for military action during the Civil War in the Milton area and for a time was guarded day and night by Federal troops.

A second Mud River Bridge stands at a different location across the river. It was built in 1876 and still remains as a tribute to the engineering of wooden bridges and to their place in the transportation network of a developing United States. The style or architecture of the structure is patterned after the innovations in the use of iron as a supporting material developed by William Howe, but this bridge also utilizes the strength of an arch, which was added in 1893.

For a long while, commerce in the central part of Cabell County depended on the valuable link across the Mud River that this second bridge provided. The town of Milton began growing and prospering with the coming of the Chesapeake and Ohio Railway in the early 1870s. Increased business activity required better means of transportation, so the Cabell County Court let a contract to build a wooden bridge across the Mud River in late 1874. The local postmaster won at least part of the job, and he and his crew finished work by late 1875 or early 1876, despite high water in the spring. The bridge's prominence as a landmark became immediately clear, for when the town of Milton was incorporated in 1876, its boundary listing began "at the south side of the Milton bridge across the Mud River."

This bridge's design, basically that devised by William Howe in about 1840, incorporating "X"-truss in wooden beams and the major vertical supports in iron tie rods rather than wood. The Mud River Bridge carries the basic design a little further, though, doubling the trusses with two sets of crossbeams placed between each set of tie rods with a wooden arch providing additional strength. The bridge is 112 feet long overall and 14 feet wide and rests on cut stone abutments.

This bridge increased the flow of commerce and greatly

Mr. and Mrs. Sampson Sanders Simmons standing at the entrance to the Mud River Bridge. MARSHALL UNIVERSITY ARCHIVE, F.B. LAMBERT COLLECTION

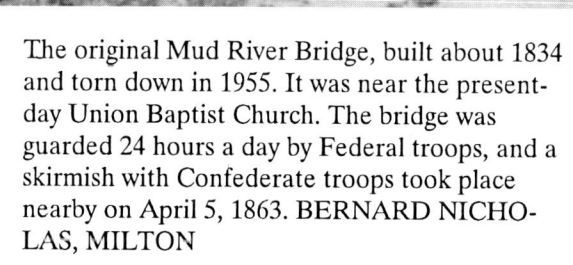

The original Mud River Bridge, built about 1834 and torn down in 1955. It was near the present-day Union Baptist Church. The bridge was guarded 24 hours a day by Federal troops, and a skirmish with Confederate troops took place nearby on April 5, 1863. BERNARD NICHOLAS, MILTON

improved the transportation system in central Cabell County. Although it was built about the time of the laying of the Chesapeake and Ohio Railway track through the area — a time when long-distance traffic from east and west on the old James River and Kanawha Turnpike, where the original bridge stood, was much diminished — it facilitated the movement of goods and people to the railroad depots and into the surrounding countryside.

Maintenance records from 1891 show the importance of this structure to the area's commerce inasmuch as the court paid $110.09 for needed repairs. Since this bridge is located in an area of steep banks and rough terrain, fording the stream would have been difficult, and people must have appreciated the convenience of this link in their road system.

From the time of construction until 1971, this second bridge apparently underwent only minor repairs. In 1971, however, the West Virginia Department of Highways, the agency responsible for maintenance, undertook the task of structural restoration at the urging of the Covered Bridge Garden Club of Milton. Although this second bridge was completely renovated, it was not replaced as the original bridge on the Kanawha Turnpike had been. Care was taken not to destroy the integrity of design, and beams in need of replacement or repair were matched for size and placed in the original positions. The bridge floor is now underpinned with steel girders, and extra steel abutments have been added. New siding and a new floor were constructed, the roof supports were completely removed and a new roof was built. The structure was upgraded to handle common loads so that it remains in use, but it is in poor condition.

Exterior view. This is the post-Civil War structure and not the older bridge that the sign indicates. HPU

Interior view. HPU

Mud River Bridge

Philippi Bridge
BARBOUR COUNTY

Location: U.S. 250 at Philippi, across the Tygart Valley River.
Truss type: Long
Length: 285' 10"
Width: 26'

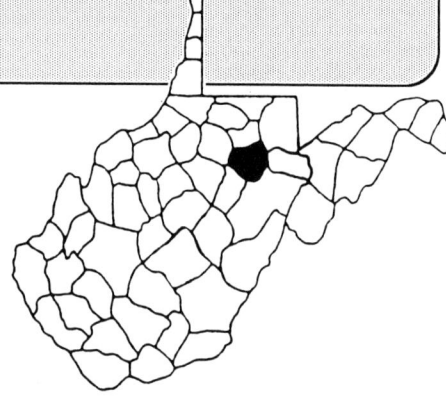

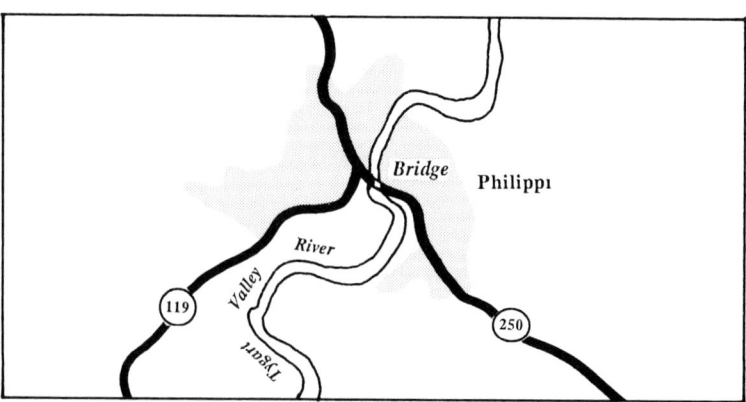

The wooden, two-span covered bridge, crossing the Tygart Valley River at Philippi, Barbour County, was built in 1852. It is one of only six remaining two-lane covered bridges in the United States. It is the oldest and longest overall covered bridge in the state and one of two remaining in Barbour County.

The bridge was built in 1851-52 to facilitate use of the 1848 Beverly and Fairmont Road, which was built to stimulate use of the Staunton-Parkersburg Turnpike as a western Virginia link with Richmond and Norfolk. The Beverly and Fairmont Road ended at Fairmont, on the Monongahela River, an important point on the new Baltimore and Ohio Railroad, which was nearing completion in the western section of the state.

The *Clarksburg Democrat* in May 1850 printed a request for bids for the bridge at Philippi. Contracts were awarded to Emmett J. O'Brien for the masonry work and to Lemuel and Eli Chenoweth, of Beverly, Va., (now West Virginia), for the superstructure. The foundation proved to be a bigger project than was originally expected, and an outbreak of typhoid fever delayed the progress further. Late in 1852 the bridge was completed at a cost of $12,181.24. The east abutment has been rebuilt.

The Philippi Bridge figured in 1861 in an early campaign of the Civil War in western Virginia. Union Gen. George B. McClellan, in Cincinnati, concerned over Confederate raids against the Baltimore and Ohio Railroad and the destruction of bridges in western Virginia, sent Ohio and Indiana troops into the region to secure the B&O for the Union. Confederate Col. George Porterfield commanded a group of local militia and cavalry with headquarters in Philippi. Learning of the movement of Union troops, Porterfield prepared to retreat to the South but delayed too long. On June 2 and 3, 1861, the Union forces, under Col. Benjamin F. Kelley, caught up with the retreating Confederates, and a brief skirmish ensued, resulting in three casualties. Confederate troops, some of

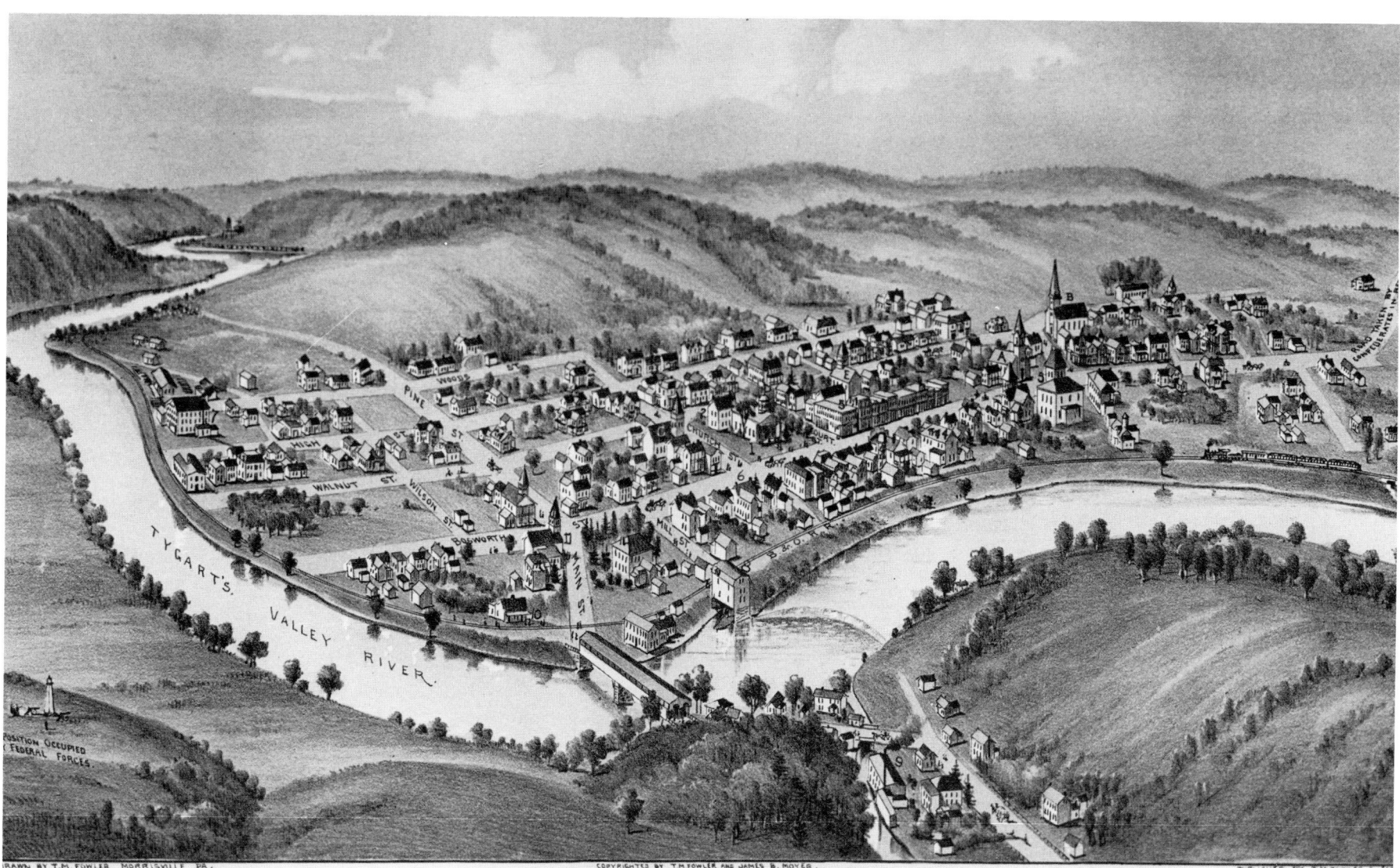

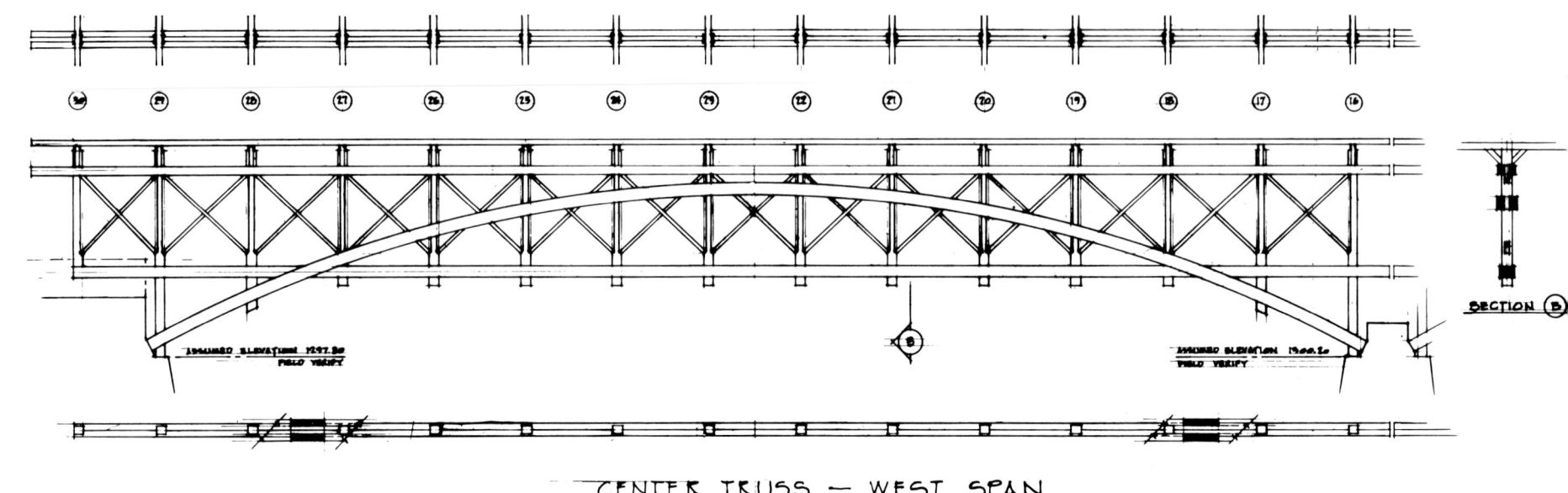

CENTER TRUSS — WEST SPAN

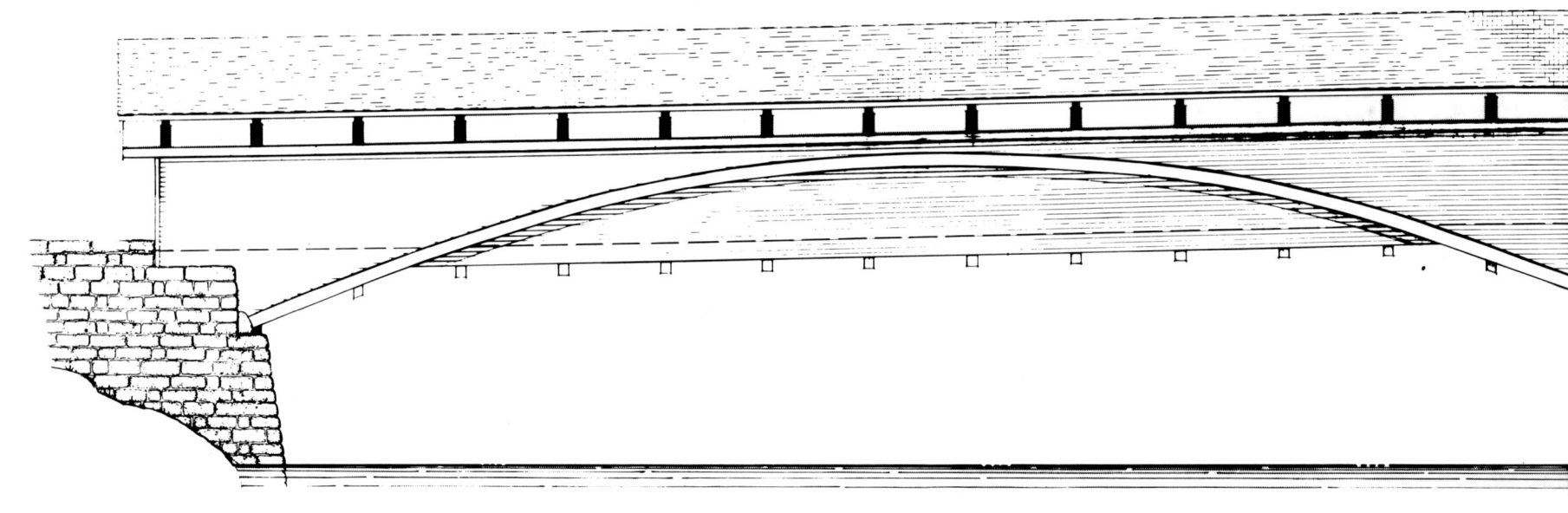

SIDE

PHILIPPI COVERED BRIDGE 1861

WEST VIRGINIA DEPARTMENT OF HIGHWAYS

WEST VIRGINIA UNIVERSITY
History of Science and Technology
in association with
PAUL D. MARSHALL and ASSOCIATES, INC.

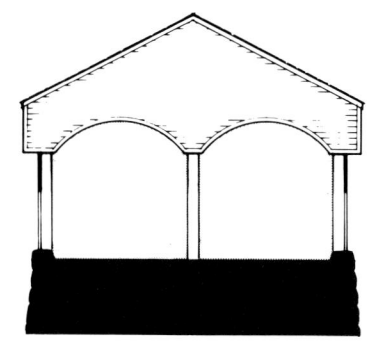

END PORTAL

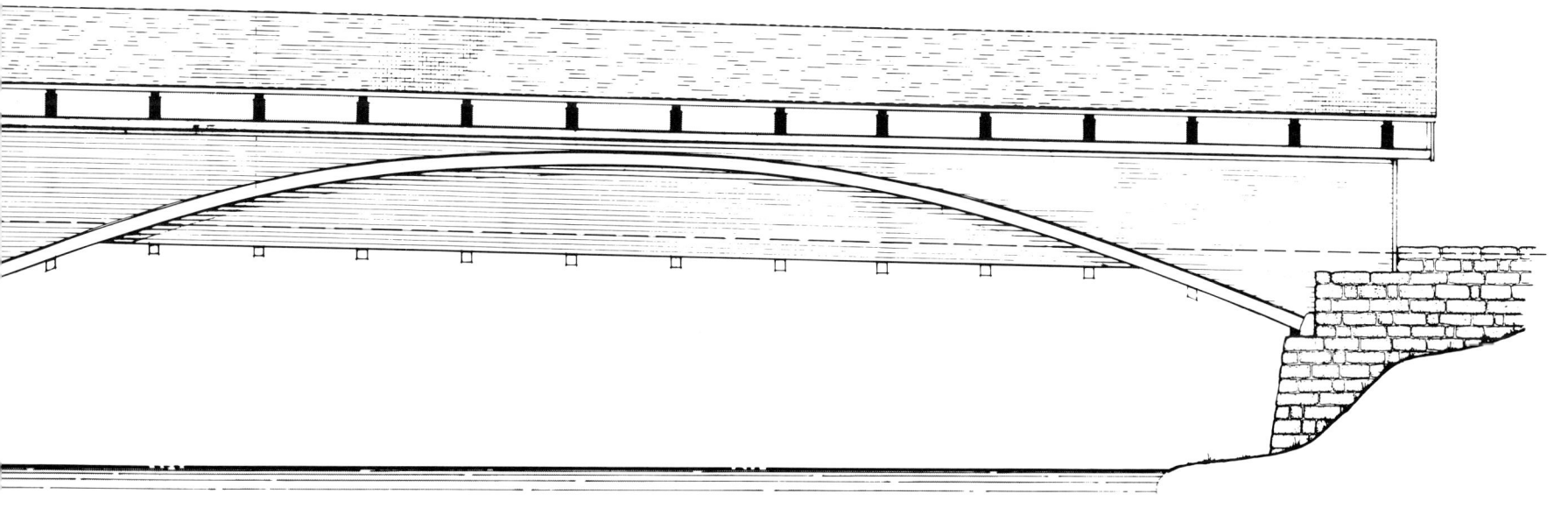

VIEW

whom were sleeping within the covered bridge, hastily fled. Colonel Dumont's 7th Indiana Volunteers captured the bridge for the Union. McClellan's reports of the affair sent to Washington were so glowing that the engagement was hailed as a major Union victory. This first inland engagement of the Civil War and the later six-day battle near Belington did, in large part, secure the B&O and this section of western Virginia for the Union cause.

Wartime traffic flowed over the bridge as supplies were moved from the railroad at Webster, south along the Tygart Valley, to maintain the army of occupation. Union troops also used the bridge as a barracks at times. Many of the other Chenoweth bridges on the Staunton Road were destroyed, and the Philippi Bridge remained intact largely because it was controlled by Union forces.

Reportedly, the bridge was in danger at two other times during the war. In 1863 the Confederate raider, Gen. William Jones, made plans to burn it, but a local citizen, Rev. Joshua Corder, convinced Jones to spare it. Then in 1864 three members of the Confederate Company D, 20th Virginia Mounted Infantry were ordered to destroy the bridge. Their commander, Brig. Gen. W.L. Jackson rescinded the order when it was learned that their plans were known by the opposition, and the risk would be too great.

Although the bridge has stood since 1852, it has been damaged many times by large, heavy coal trucks passing through the small entrance and over the floor boards which were meant to support wagons, horses and buggies.

By the late 1930s it was apparent that something had to be done, and in 1938 a new concrete floor was laid, supported by 133 tons of steel beams and two extra piers. A walkway was also added.

The big trucks inflicted further damage in 1949 and 1950, and therefore restrictions were placed on use of the bridge.

Numerous floods on the Tygart Valley River have also threatened the Philippi Bridge. In 1888 water came within two or three feet of the floor, and boards had to be removed on the side to relieve pressure from the driftwood that was accumulating. The disastrous flood of November 1985 also threatened the bridge and caused some damage.

The bridge in the 1920s. The two concrete piers were not added until 1938. SWV

The bridge in the 1950s. The two concrete piers, placed to reinforce the new concrete deck, were added in 1938. The walkway was also added at this time. SWV

West entrance to the bridge in the 1950s. SWV

Scenes of the disastrous fire of November 1989. *BARBOUR DEMOCRAT*

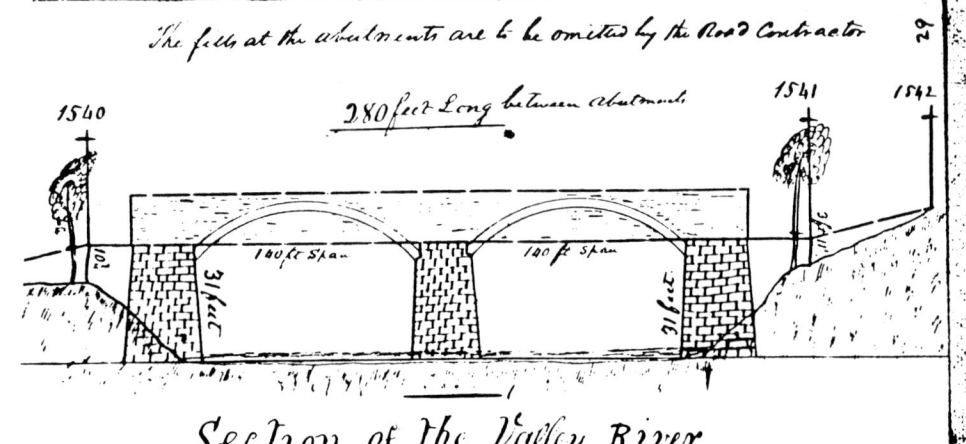

Section of the Valley River

Bridge to be built 31 feet above the bottom of the River, This being two feet higher than the great flood of 1846.

Restoration of the Historic Philippi Covered Bridge*

On Feb. 2, 1989, the historic bridge was consumed in a fireball as the result of a bizarre accident. A gasoline truck was filling the tanks of a nearby service station and convenience store when the tanker overfilled the underground tanks and pumped what was estimated to have been 1,500 gallons of gasoline onto the bridge. Because of the drainage system, virtually all of this spill ended up on the downstream lane of the bridge. For perhaps an hour, this pool of gasoline was tracked back and forth by the traveling public who were quite unaware that the liquid was gasoline and not water. Finally, the catalytic converter of a small car ignited the gasoline. The fire spread with great rapidity, resulting in the loss of the roof and the siding and heavy charring of the main structural elements. Within days of this tragic event, the governor appeared in Philippi and announced that the bridge would be rebuilt. Shortly after this announcement, Fred Van Kirk, commissioner of the West Virginia Division of Highways, invited Emory Kemp to take charge of this large-scale restoration project. The work subsequently proceeded in a series of phases.

The first phase was to clean off between half to three-quarters of an inch of char on the main structural members, to remove what little remained of the roof and siding, and to prepare drawings of the main structural members to serve as the basis of a structural analysis to see which members could be used in their burned-out condition and repaired, and which members were so badly damaged that they would have to be replaced with new material. The cleaning was undertaken by District Seven of the Division of Highways. Sandblasting had been used on earlier fire-damaged structures to remove char from both metal and wood. Thus, the cleaning started with very gentle sandblasting, but that was quickly converted to the use of simple high pressure water jets.

The architectural and engineering team consisted of Emory Kemp as chief engineer, Paul D. Marshall as preservation architect and R.R. Houston as senior preservation specialist. Although the professional team of architects and engineer were charged with the preparation of preservation plans and specifications with the intention of letting the work out to contract, it soon became obvious that it would be very difficult to prepare such documents without a detailed knowledge of the condition of all the members after the trusses had been disassembled. Equally important, it was determined that there were no bridge contractors in the region who could undertake this work and produce a rebuilt bridge according to the secretary of the interior's standards for historic preservation. Thus, in the spring of 1989, it was decided that West Virginia University, through the Institute for the History of Technology and Industrial Archaeology, should undertake the rebuilding of the bridge on a "turn-key" basis. With this approach, all of the design work, drawings and specifications, as well as the actual work, would be undertaken by the Institute.

During the spring of 1989, a town meeting was held in which a nearly unanimous vote was received from the local population that the bridge should be restored to its condition of June 3, 1861, when the first land battle of the Civil War occurred at the site. It was also determined to address the 1938 reconstruction of the bridge, which consisted of cutting out the original deck and building a bridge within a bridge, that is, installing a reinforced concrete deck supported on continuous steel girders running nearly 308 feet from end to end of the bridge. This concrete bridge had been cast around all the truss members in the bridge, and thus, in order to repair and replace fire-damaged members, it was necessary to remove the deck, but leave the girders, which could support a working platform under the bridge. A contract was let to Heavy Structures, Inc., to remove the deck and the sidewalk installed in 1938. The work was completed at the end of November 1989.

While the work of removing the deck and cleaning up the

---

*Excerpted from the winter issue of the Institute for the History of Technology and Industrial Archaeology newsletter.

site was underway, a preservation plan was developed by the professional team. It was determined that the condition of the bridge in 1861 was quite different from that after its reconstruction in 1938. Information from archives as well as archaeological information from the structure itself indicated that the bridge had had horizontal siding and that the arches had protruded from the siding, while the roof, rather than having a rolled asphalt cover, originally was of poplar shingles painted barn red to protect them from the weather. A noticeable change was the alteration of the end gables to provide extra clearance for coal trucks, completely altering the original appearance of the bridge, which had two curved openings in the gable over the traffic lanes.

The Institute received its contract in December 1989, and began work on the site in February after it recruited a team of workmen in the categories of laborer, carpenter's helper, carpenter, and various specialists and superintendents. All of these job descriptions had to be prepared and approved through West Virginia University, since these employees were to become part of the university system.

Early in the autumn of 1989, the West Virginia Forestry Association agreed to provide all of the yellow poplar to rebuild the bridge, a commitment of approximately 185,000 board feet. The bridge was constructed entirely of yellow poplar, wood which would be used not only for repairing and replacing main structural elements, but used also for the siding, roof and shingles. During the late winter of 1990, a canopy of wooden arches and heavy-duty plastic sheathing was constructed over the bridge to provide a more controlled environment for epoxy repair of members and the preparation by hand of various timber joints, since this work required dry conditions. Although the canopy was damaged twice by storms and threatened by several floods, it proved its worth over the length of the project. As of Oct. 1, 1990, it was estimated that it saved 116 working days in which inclement weather would have closed down the job.

The first logs arrived from the Forestry Association in April 1990 and were sent to a sawmill in Belington, where a bandsaw was modified to receive logs up to 60 feet long. Most of the wood for the bridge, including large timber members, planks and other smaller components, was cut at this mill, however some material was sawn by Dingess Lumber Company of Belington as well. The sawn material was sent to the bridge site, where it was cut to size, with mortise and tenon joints prepared according to original specifications. During the course of reconstruction, it was necessary to disassemble all of the trusses and arches in the bridge, and in so doing it was found that the lower chord, which had not been burnt because of its location below the reinforced concrete deck, had deteriorated heavily because of rot and insect infestation. Therefore, all of the members had to be carefully prepared with newly developed epoxy treatment, with reinforcement added where necessary. The amount of reinforcement was determined by a structural analysis of the supporting members, with each member evaluated to see whether it could sustain the forces which would be required for expected live loads in the future, when the original deck would be reinstalled in the bridge. The lower chords provided an important challenge because they sustained heavy tensile loads, necessitating the addition of steel reinforcement at weakened sections and through the innumerable joints and splices encountered in the lower chords. The work proceeded steadily after the arrival of the first logs in April 1990.

The professionals involved in the bridge also provided engineering and architectural design for phase three of the bridge work. This consisted of repair and repositioning of the steel girders, the installation of a new timber deck, the complete redesign of the drainage system and the reconstruction of the intersection at the west end of the bridge, together with the installation of overhead traffic barriers to prevent heavy trucks from entering the bridge from either end. And finally, work on the structure included a new sprinkling system with fire detectors as well as security and interpretive lighting. The bridge was finished and reopened to traffic in the summer of 1991.

Philippi Bridge

Canopy.

Removed char – set up for repair.

Repair work with epoxy on upright columns.

Front view of the completed bridge showing the height barrier for trucks.

Interior of the completed bridge.

Photos courtesy Paul Marshall and Gordon Blair Lee

Repair work on bottom chord of upstream truss.

Upstream truss undergoing restoration.

Sarvis Fork Bridge
JACKSON COUNTY

Location: On County Route 21/15 just off County Route 21, 1.2 miles north of Sandyville. Crosses left Fork of Sandy Creek.
Truss type: Long
Length: 101' 3-1/2"
Width: 11' 8"

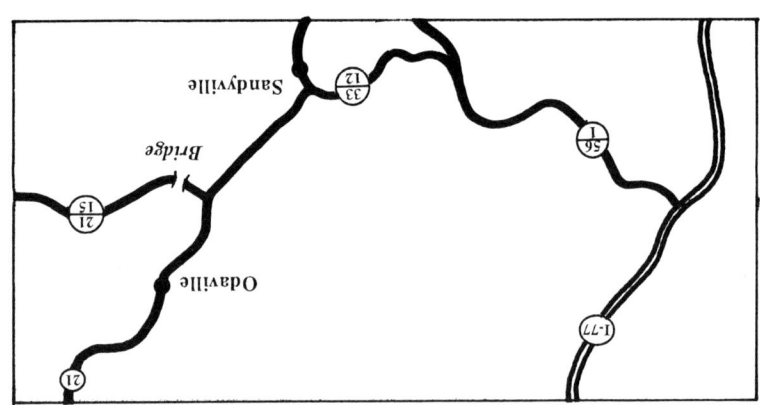

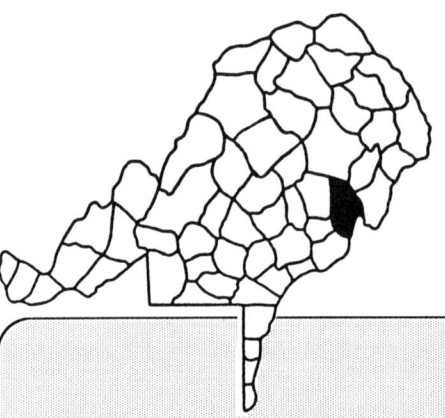

The Sarvis Fork Bridge on the Left Fork of Big Sandy Creek, Jackson County, was built in 1889 over the John Carnahan Fork, west of Ripley, on a branch of Big Mill Creek. The Jackson County Court contracted for the bridge, and the bridge, fills and approaches were constructed by George W. Staats, for $64 under contract. It was built with a modified Long system.

In 1924, during construction of U.S. Route 33, an iron bridge was built nearby and the Carnahan Bridge was abandoned. The same year the Jackson County court contracted with C.R. Kent, R.R. Hardesty and E.R. Duke "to tear down the Carnahan bridge below Ripley and rebuild the same across the Left Fork of Big Sandy Creek, near the home of William Weekley" for $1,050.

The day before Christmas, 1969, a state road truck crossing the bridge broke through the floor. The bridge was out of use for a month but shortly afterward steel beams were added to support the structure and a new floor was installed. The state-owned bridge is still in use and is in fair condition.

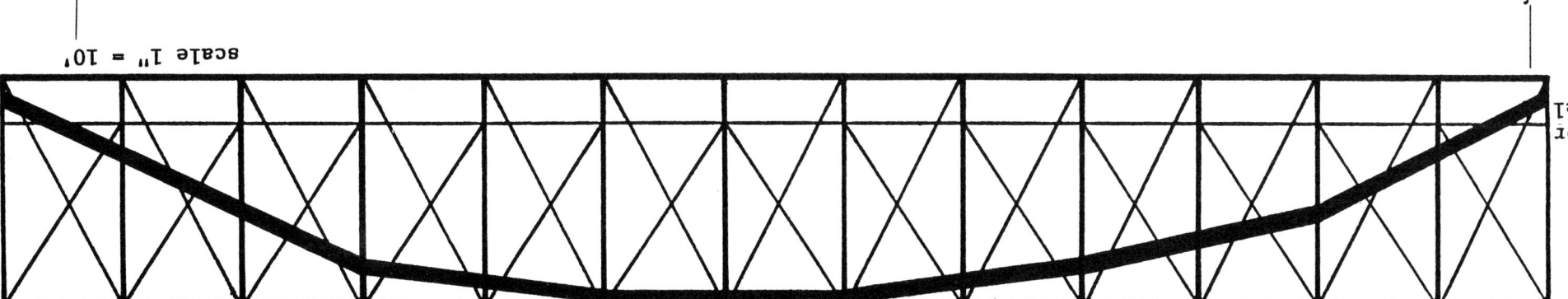

scale 1" = 10'

A modified Long system of 13 "X" panels with an arch. Each "X" is made up of three timers, measuring 6" x 7" in cross section, bolted together at the center of the "X." The arch is made up of timbers measuring 11-1/2" x 4" in cross section, bolted to the "X" panels, but is not a major structural element for the support of the bridge.

Exterior view, HPU

Interior view, HPU

PHOTO BY GERALD RATLIFF

Sarvis Fork Bridge

Simpson Creek Bridge
HARRISON COUNTY

Location: On County Route 24/2, just off County Route 24 at Exit 121 off Interstate 79. Crosses Simpson Creek.

Truss type: Multiple Kingpost
Length: 75' 2"
Width: 14' 3"

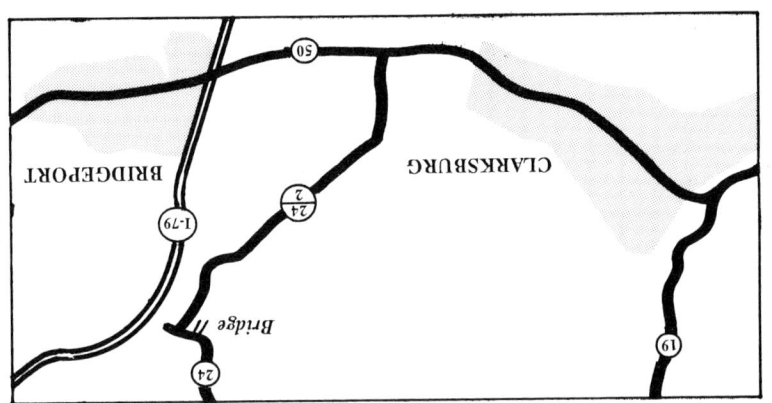

The bridge is preserved in a small park and has been bypassed by a new bridge. HPU

The W.T. Law Bridge crosses Simpson Creek, near Bridgeport, in Harrison County. It is one of two remaining bridges in the county.

In 1881 the County Court commission appointed Col. T.S. Spates to locate a site and advertise for construction of a covered bridge at Holland's Mill. Asa S. Hugill was the low bidder with a bid of $1,483. The bridge is significant because it depends on multiple Kingpost trusses rather than arches to support its 75-foot span.

The bridge was washed out by a flood in July 1889 and moved a half mile upstream to its present location. In July 1984 a tree fell across its roof during a severe thunderstorm, but repairs were made the next year with funding from the Department of Highways and the Department of Culture and History. It is owned by the state, is in use and in good condition.

According to legend, a Joseph Johnson, who settled in the Bridgeport area, laid out some lots near the first Simpson Creek Bridge, built about 1811. As he saw people crossing the bridge, he observed that it was a port or gateway to his proposed lots. This supposedly gave him the idea to combine the words and call the new town "Bridgeport."

SIMPSON CREEK BRIDGE

Staats Mill Bridge

JACKSON COUNTY

Location: FFA-FHA State Camp and Conference Center at Cedar Lakes.
Truss type: Long
Length: 97'
Width: 11' 4"

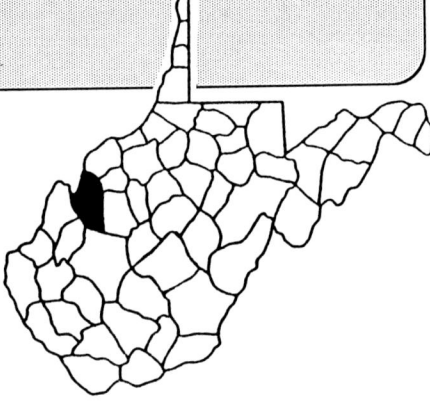

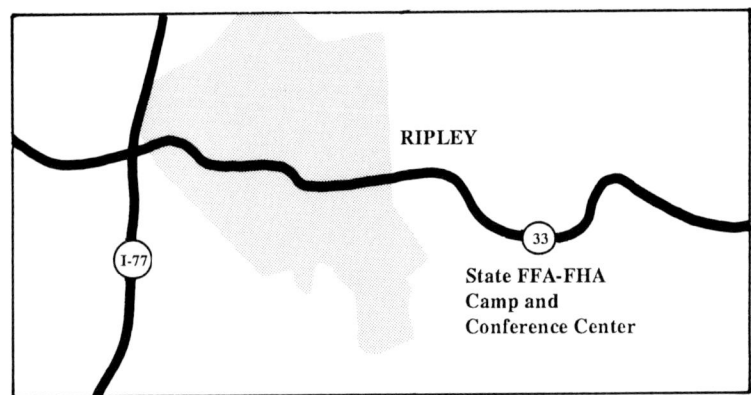

The community that came to be known as Staats Mill was founded by Abraham Staats (1750-1826), who fought in the Revolutionary War, and Ann King Staats (1755-1811). Their son, Cornelius, fought in the War of 1812 and married Ann Carney. They were the parents of Isaac Staats, who built the first water-powered mill on Tug Fork of Big Mill Creek, the site called Staats Mill. The present covered bridge was built adjacent to the mill and near a store, both owned by Isaac's son, Enoch. Thus it is apparent that the bridge site has played an important role in the history and development of Jackson County since the eighteenth century.

In 1887 the Jackson County Court, under the presidency of George W. Shinn, appointed Shinn, George I. Walker and S.M. Rader to select a site for the proposed bridge over Tug Fork of Big Mill Creek. The bridge at Hardesty's Mill over Tug Fork was adopted as a model, and the stone work was done by Quincy and Grim, local masons, at a cost of $710.40. The wood superstructure was made by local builder, H.T. Hartley for $903.95, and Enoch Staats made the dirt fills for the approaches for the sum of $110. The total cost of the Staats Mill Bridge was $1,788.35.

The bridge was constructed according to the Long system, patented by Stephen Long in 1830, but also framed without the use of stiffening arches, despite the fact that the span was nearly 100 feet. The result was, and is, an outstanding example of a pure Long Truss covered bridge of notable length, executed by craftsmen of considerable skill.

Built in 1888 the bridge is an impressive and historically significant example of a late nineteenth century timber-covered bridge. Its total length is 97 feet, excluding the overhang of the eaves, and the clear span between abutments is 85 feet, seven inches. The main structure of the bridge consists of two large timber trusses. The distinctive feature of Long Trusses are the "X"-braced diagonals in each of the panels. In the case of this covered bridge, there are 11 such panels, each eight feet, seven inches long and 14 feet, three inches deep. The timber

Staats Mill Bridge, 1887. HPU

three-span steel girders. A laminated two-by-four-inch timber deck was installed on the steel floor beams and provided with an asphalt overlay as a wearing course.

Vertical siding covers the entire truss work on both sides of the bridge except for a space under the eaves which acts as a clerestory to provide light to the inside of the bridge. It was painted the traditional barn red. It is covered with a simple pitched roof, sherardized with a standing seam metal surface supported on timber girders and rafters. Because of the large exposed side area, a horizontal truss was usually incorporated in the roof structure of covered bridges to resist lateral wind loads. These trusses traditionally consisted of transverse timbers and diagonal cross-bracing firmly secured by wooden pegs, called "treenails," and wedges. It is virtually certain that such a bracing was part of the original Staats Mill Bridge structure, but all that remains today are loosely fastened diagonals that serve little purpose in resisting lateral loads.

The abutments at the original site consisted of full-height cut stone, done locally, which support both the original trusses and the new steel girders.

In 1983 the old bridge was moved to the FFA-FHA State Camp at Cedar Lakes, three miles from the original site and reconstructed across a pond at a cost of $104,000. It is in excellent condition and open to pedestrian traffic only.

The community that came to be known as Staats Mill was founded by Abraham Staats (1750-1826), who fought in the Revolutionary War, and Ann King Staats (1755-1811). Their son, Cornelius, fought in the War of 1812 and married Ann Carney. They were the parents of Isaac Staats, who built the first water-powered mill on Tug Fork of Big Mill Creek, the site called Staats Mill. The present covered bridge was built adjacent to the mill and near a store, both owned by Isaac's son, Enoch. Thus it is apparent that the bridge site has played an important role in the history and development of Jackson County since the eighteenth century.

In 1887 the Jackson County Court, under the presidency of George W. Shinn, appointed Shinn, George I. Walker and S.M. Rader to select a site for the proposed bridge over Tug Fork of Big Mill Creek. The bridge at Hardesty's Mill over Tug Fork was adopted as a model, and the stone work was done by Quincy and Grim, local masons, at a cost of $710.40. The wood superstructure was made by local builder, H.T. Hartley for $903.95, and Enoch Staats made the dirt fills for the approaches for the sum of $110. The total cost of the Staats Mill Bridge was $1,788.35.

The bridge was constructed according to the Long system, patented by Stephen Long in 1830, but also framed without the use of stiffening arches, despite the fact that the span was nearly 100 feet. The result was, and is, an outstanding example of a pure Long Truss covered bridge of notable length, executed by craftsmen of considerable skill.

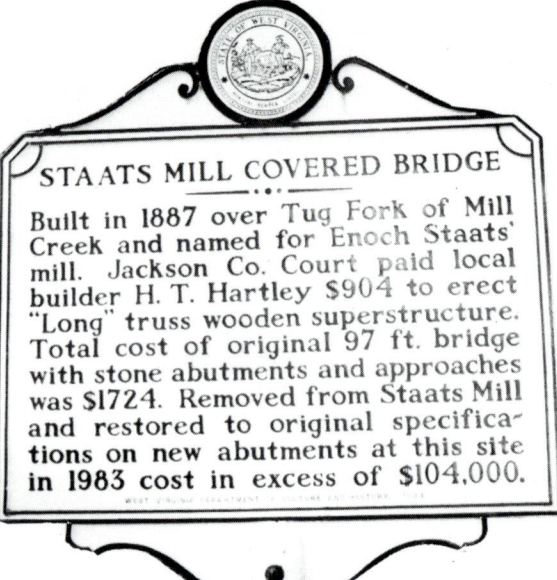

Exterior view. HPU

The bridge was moved as a result of a major flood control and water supply project by the U.S. Soil Conservation Service.

Interior views. HPU

Staats Mill Bridge

Walkersville Bridge

LEWIS COUNTY

Location: Just off U.S. 19, one mile south of Walkersville across the right fork of the West Fork River.
Truss type: Queenpost
Length: 39' 4"
Width: 12' 1-1/2"

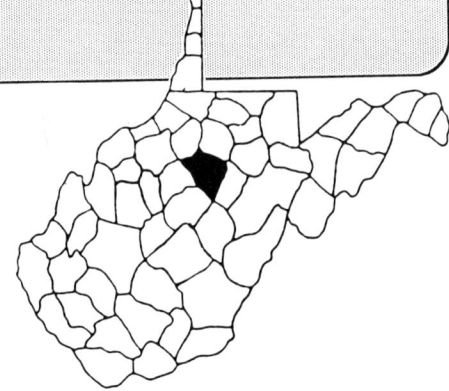

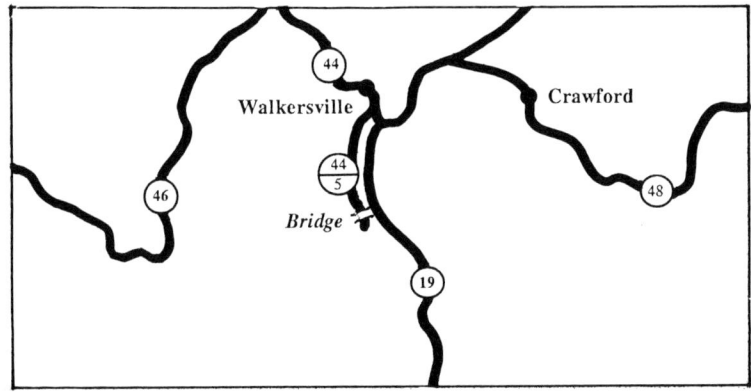

The only remaining bridge in Lewis County spans the right fork of the West Fork River. It was built in 1903 by John G. Sprigg for $567 in the Queenpost Truss design. The bridge is still in use, is in good condition and is owned by the state.

Exterior view. MIKE KELLER

Walkersville Bridge

THE OLD COVERED BRIDGE

The old covered bridge, grown decrepit and gray
In the battle of years, has now passed away;
For Time, the remorseless, has triumphed at last,
And the old wooden bridge is a thing of the past.
Like a warrior it stood, with its feet in the tide,
Its arms welcoming travelers from far and from wide.

When the fiercest storms raged, and loud thunderbolts fell,
Like arrows out flung from the portals of hell;
When the fury of wind sent a chill to the blood,
And the highway of man was a gateway of flood;
Then the old covered bridge strained its sinews of wood,
And tottered, and quivered, but stiffened and stood!

At night time, in winter, when snow drifts lay deep,
And the wind was awake and the world was asleep;
Or in summer, when housetop, and hilltop and stream
Were alight with the touch of the moon's silver beam;
Then the old wooden bridge, with arms outstretched wide,
Like a sentinel, guarded the slumbering tide.

Oh, the old covered bridge knew the heartbreak and tears
Of the travelers who crossed it, their sorrows and fears!
And it shared, also, in their pastimes and joys —
Knew the happy farm girls and jolly farm boys!
But there came one day, in its hundredth year,
Sent by Time, the despoiler, who rules this vast sphere,
A shining young knight in a girder of steel,
And the old bridge fell under the conqueror's heel.

by Alma Dudding
from 1951 Scrapbook

Section II

Bridges Gone and Forgotten in West Virginia

The Middle Fork Bridge, which was the site of one of the earliest Civil War skirmishes fought in this part of the state. The bridge, spanning the Middle Fork River on the line between Barbour and Upshur counties, carried traffic over the important Staunton-Parkersburg Turnpike during the war. The skirmish occurred on July 6-7, 1861, between a small force of Federals and a company of Confederate pickets guarding the bridge. The Federals were repulsed with one dead and five wounded. SWV

The bridge across the Little Kanawha River at Bulltown in Braxton County. This important central West Virginia covered bridge was erected in 1850. Bulltown was a center for salt furnaces and supplied salt to a large part of northwest Virginia until the Civil War. During the war it was used by both sides and was the scene of one major skirmish on Oct. 13, 1863. The bridge was torn down in the 1940s. SWV

The original bridge over Middle Island Creek at West Union, Doddridge County. This long bridge was designed by Lewis Wernwag and built in the 1830s along the Northwestern Turnpike, which is now U.S. 50. A new bridge was built, and the covered bridge was restricted to pedestrian traffic after 1941, but in June of 1950 a swollen creek washed the bridge off its foundations and deposited it against the new concrete bridge. WVU

Top Right: The first bridge across the Gauley River at Gauley Bridge, Fayette County, was constructed in 1822 on the James River and Kanawha Turnpike. It was destroyed by fire in 1826, and the second covered bridge (pictured) was built on the same site in 1850. This bridge was burned by retreating Confederate forces on July 27, 1861. FAYETTE COUNTY HISTORICAL SOCIETY

Middle: This temporary suspension bridge was built in early 1862 by Federal troops on the old covered bridge piers across Gauley River. It was in turn burned by the Federals on their retreat from Gauley Bridge in September 1862. There was not another bridge built across the Gauley River until 1925. WVU

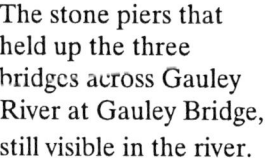

The stone piers that held up the three bridges across Gauley River at Gauley Bridge, still visible in the river.

The Greenbrier River Bridge at Caldwell, Greenbrier County, built in 1875 to replace an earlier bridge destroyed during the Civil War. This was the last remaining covered bridge on the Midland Trail in West Virginia when it was torn down in 1932. The old inn, Elmhurst, which is still in existence, sits at the east end of the original bridge site. GREENBRIER COUNTY HISTORICAL SOCIETY.

The Falling Springs Bridge at Renick, Greenbrier County, as it looked in 1930. At 332 feet, it was perhaps one of the longest ever built in the state. It crossed the Greenbrier River at this small town north of Lewisburg. Built in the late 1880s, the bridge stood until a violent storm destroyed it on May 2, 1935, injuring two women who had taken shelter in it. POCAHONTAS COUNTY HISTORICAL SOCIETY

Bridge at "Eastview," three miles from Alderson, Greenbrier County, on the old Blue Sulphur Springs Turnpike over Muddy Creek. It was replaced in the 1940s by the Cline Bridge. GREENBRIER COUNTY HISTORICAL SOCIETY

The Bridges of Harrison County

Bridges at Marshville, Harrison County, about 1920. The Ten Mile Bridge, foreground, was built in 1885 and rebuilt in 1893 after burning. The Grass Run Bridge, background, was built in 1883. SWV

Harrison County

The original Pine Bluff Bridge in Harrison County, built in the mid-1850s. Apparently it was replaced in the late 1800s by another covered bridge which lasted until the 1930s. The Pine Bluff community was originally called Shinn's Mill after Moses Shinn, who built a mill there about 1835. SWV

The second Sardis Bridge was built in 1879 replacing the original bridge of 1861. It crossed the Left Hand Fork of Ten Mile Creek and was 75 feet long. This bridge, too, was replaced in 1955. WVU

This bridge, built in 1900 next to the home of Dow Martin, crossed Bingamon Creek near Shinnston, Harrison County. It was replaced in 1949. SWV

Harrison County

The Upper Brushy Fork bridge was contracted for by Asa S. Hugill, lowest bidder, for $600. When Hugill failed to furnish the required bond, the contract was then let to John Greathouse for $675. Greathouse completed the bridge in 1893. It was 28 feet long and 14 feet wide. It has been replaced by a modern structure. WVU

The Horab Bridge, named for the nearby Horab Church. It was built in 1875 across Elk Creek, and was extensively repaired in 1882. Then the flood of 1888 washed it away, but it was rebuilt and continued in use until it collapsed under the weight of a coal truck in 1952. WVU

The Dola Bridge. It crossed the Right Hand Fork of Ten Mile Creek and was built in 1890 for $1700. It was 64 feet long. WVU

Harrison County

The Lloyd L. Lang Bridge, which crossed the Brushy Fork of Elk Creek. It was built in 1885 and was 45 feet long and 14 feet wide. WVU

The Fletcher Bridge across Ten Mile Creek north of U.S. 50 near Marshville. It was built in 1891 and was 62 feet long. WVU

The Kinchelo Creek Bridge was built in 1877 and crossed the Lewis-Harrison County line. WVU

The Maulsby Bridge was the longest and best-known covered bridge in Harrison County. It was built about 1848 across the West Fork River. The 300-foot bridge was built by the Weston and Fairmont Turnpike Company, connecting these two towns in central West Virginia. This bridge figured prominently in Confederate Gen. William E. Jones' raid in April 1863 through this part of the state. WVU

Harrison County

The Margaret Bridge in the extreme northwestern corner of the county at the village of Margaret crossed Quaker Fork. It was 32 feet long and was built in 1893. WVU

The Jarvisville Bridge crossed over the Left Hand Fork of Ten Mile Creek at Jarvisville. It was built in 1875 but washed away in 1896. It was retrieved and put back on its abutments. WVU

The Jesse Kennedy Bridge crossed Lost Creek near the town of Lost Creek. It was built about 1882. WVU

The Porter Maxwell Bridge crossed Gnatty Creek, the largest branch of Elk Creek. The first bridge was built in 1874. The second bridge was built in 1887 and dismantled in the early 1950s. It was 25 feet long. WVU

Harrison County

Bridge across Rooting Creek. On May 2, 1887, the Harrison County Court appointed James M. Eib, a county commissioner, to examine the bridge across Rooting Creek, just south of Romines Mills in Harrison County. The county wanted to replace it with a covered bridge similar to one that spanned Lost Creek. Eib contracted with George C. Blair to construct the bridge, using the Kingpost Truss design, for $675. The bridge was completed on Oct. 6, 1887, and was 12 feet, 1-1/2 inches wide and 31.4 feet long. It had red board-and-batten siding and later a corrugated metal roof. The only recent alterations to the bridge were concrete and woodwork added to the abutments. On Nov. 22, 1979, vandals set fire to the bridge and practically destroyed it. It was disassembled and is now in storage.

Extensive damage caused by the 1979 fire. The siding and roof were lost and there was deep charring of the main trusses. HPU

An artist's conception of the first bridge built across the Coal River at what it now St. Albans, Kanawha County. A sign on each end of the bridge reads: "Turn to the right as the law directs. A fine of $5.00 for passing faster than a walk." The bridge was built in 1830 by Phillip Roots Thompson and Stephen Teays to accommodate the James River & Kanawha Turnpike, and was destroyed by Confederate troops in July 1861 on their retreat from the area, which was called Coalsmouth at the time. The present-day Main Street Bridge now occupies the place where the old bridge stood.
PAUL MARSHALL & ASSOCIATES

The covered bridge at Romney, Hampshire County, across the South Branch of the Potomac River. Federal troops crossed the bridge during the June 13, 1861 battle between the Confederates and Co. Lewis Wallace's Eleventh Indiana Regiment. Wallace's run across the bridge resulted in the rout of the Confederates from Romney. *HARPER'S WEEKLY*

This is the second bridge built in central West Virginia by Lemuel Chenoweth. Built in 1854, it crossed Stove Coal Creek at the "Maxwell Ford" in Lewis County, one mile west of Weston on the Staunton and Parkersburg Turnpike. Much Civil War action occurred in the vicinity. There is no record of when the bridge was removed. WVU

The Lightburn Bridge, built in the 1870s and replaced in 1928. The bridge was almost washed away in the flood of 1888, but was saved by four men who risked their lives to clear away trees and debris that had lodged against it. WVU

Another Chenoweth bridge, built in 1853-54 across the West Fork River, south of Weston in Lewis County. It was about 100 feet long, and during the Civil War was important to both sides for troop movement. The bridge was saved from the ravages of the flood of 1888 when its sides were removed to let the water rush through. In 1911-12 the bridge was reinforced and continued in use until 1953 when it was destroyed. SWV

Three views of one of the older bridges in Marion County. It crossed Paw Paw Creek near Grant Town and was 48 feet long. HPU

The old Durbannah Bridge, which was torn down in 1897. It crossed Decker's Creek in Morgantown, Monongalia County, near the present downtown area. WVU

Taking down the Greenbrier River Bridge at Marlinton in 1915. POCAHONTAS COUNTY HISTORICAL SOCIETY VIA BILL McNEEL

This covered bridge was located at Huntersville across Knapps Creek on the original road between that community and Dunmore. Contracts for the bridge were let by the County Court in June 1887. In May 1889 high water in Knapps Creek damaged the abutments on the bridge. The Court first planned to repair the bridge but then decided to rebuilt it at a new site a short distance upstream. The bridge was replaced in 1909 with a steel bridge. POCAHONTAS COUNTY HISTORICAL SOCIETY

The original Greenbrier River Bridge, at Marlinton, Pocahontas County, built in 1854-56 by Lemuel Chenoweth. It was the first bridge across the river at this site and was engineered by a man named Haymond, who also engineered the Lewisburg and Marlinton Turnpike and the Huttonsville and Marlinton Turnpike. During the Civil War both armies used the bridge, but it was spared destruction. In 1915 the bridge was dismantled and a concrete structure put in its place. This bridge in turn was replaced by the present structure in late 1959. POCAHONTAS COUNTY HISTORICAL SOCIETY VIA BILL McNEEL

The original Cheat River Bridge, one of the longest covered bridges in the state. It spanned the Cheat River, five miles south of Rowlesburg, Preston County, near the tiny community of Macomber on what is now U.S. 50. The bridge was built around 1834 by Josiah Kidwell and was paid for with money raised in a lottery and the sale of shares. Tolls were charged for many years to pay for the upkeep. Timbers for the huge 339-foot, two-lane span were cut from massive white pine trees in Tucker County and floated down the Cheat River to the bridge site. On April 27, 1863, Confederate Gen. William E. Jones brought his army into Preston County on his famous raid through the northern part of the state. Two thousand troops crossed over the bridge, tearing up the flooring on one side to impede the progress of the pursuing Federal troops. It was nearly two years before repairs were made so that two-way traffic could move across the bridge again. The years continued to take their toll, and in 1934, a new bridge was built a short distance downstream to handle U.S. 50 traffic. The covered bridge was then closed to vehicular traffic. A new roof was put on, and the bridge remained in reasonably good condition until 1964 when it caught fire and was totally destroyed. SWV

SWV

Part of the original middle pier is still standing.

-103-

Putnam County

The 18-Mile Creek Bridge, near Buffalo, Putnam County, built in 1884. WILLIAM WINTZ

Buxton's Mill and covered bridge across 13-Mile Creek near Buffalo, Putnam County. The mill was built in 1877 and the 150-foot bridge in 1887. An iron bridge replaced it in 1949. WILLIAM WINTZ

Putnam County

The Cross Creek Bridge at the lower end of Buffalo, Putnam County. WILLIAM WINTZ

The bridge across the Poca River in Putnam County. Route 62 crosses here now. The bridge was torn down about 1920. WILLIAM WINTZ

The old McKinney Bridge, which spanned the North Fork of Hughes River near Cairo in Ritchie County. Built in 1878, it was the first covered bridge over the Hughes River. Years later it was replaced by a new bridge, and on Sept. 3, 1970, it collapsed and fell into the river. WVU

A pier from the Fetterman Bridge at Grafton, Taylor County. Until it was destroyed by the flood of 1888, this bridge was the oldest covered bridge in the county, built in 1834-35 and carrying traffic across the Tygart Valley River and the important Northwestern Turnpike. This was an important locale for both sides during the Civil War, and the first Federal soldier killed, Thornsberry Bailey Brown, died near the entrance to the bridge on May 22, 1961. AUTHOR'S COLLECTION

About the Author

Stan Cohen is a native of Charleston and a graduate of West Virginia University with a degree in geology. After spending many years working as a consulting geologist, owning a ski shop and as director of a historical museum, he established Pictorial Histories Publishing Company in 1976. Since then he has authored or co-authored 40 books and published over 140. He specializes in pictorial history subjects and is a major national publisher of military books and the largest publisher of West Virginia history books. His West Virginia titles include: The Civil War in West Virginia; West Virginia's Civil War Sites; Historic Sites of West Virginia; King Coal; Historic Springs of the Virginias; Kanawha County Images; Roar Lions Roar and Capitols of West Virginia as well as 12 other titles by West Virginia authors.

About the Artist

Linda J.C. Turner works primarily in watercolor and pen and ink. Her paintings and drawings reflect her interests in people, history and nature. She has received many awards for her work which can be found in private and corporate collections across the United States.

Turner teaches art classes and workshops, is actively involved in arts, history and cultural projects, has been listed in Who's Who in W.Va., and is a co-founder of the West Virginia Watercolor Society.

A native West Virginian, she spent many childhood years traveling with her family because of her father's Air Force career. She is a graduate of Glenville State College and taught art, basic skills, and science in public schools for seven years. She then began working full time as an artist, establishing her Laurelwood Studio in Jane Lew, W.Va., where she and her husband and daughter make their home.

About the Cover Painting and Limited Edition Print

"Philippi Bridge – Spring 1861" portrays the covered bridge in late May, just days before the event heralding the Conflict which would rend a state in two and plunge a nation into years of despair. Before peace returned, the bridge would witness passage of both Union and Confederate troops and supplies, many times. The appearance of the bridge remained greatly altered until the restoration of 1991.

In April 1989, Linda J.C. Turner was commissioned by Project Manager, chief historian and engineer, Dr. Emory Kemp, and by historical architects, Paul D. Marshall & Associates, Inc., and R. Richmond "Sam" Houston, restoration specialist, to develop a painting of the Philippi Covered Bridge, as it stood in 1861. Research began, and in a few weeks Turner had completed a preliminary painting which the architects presented before the Restoration Committee in May 1989, as a facsimile of the proposed restoration.

The artist began a careful study of the bridge, measuring and sketching the various members and joints. The surfaces of the arches and chords had to be searched carefully for the correct nail holes and mortices, indicating the position of wall studs and the spacing of siding. An unexpected finding made by Turner, was that the lower chord of the truss had been exposed when the bridge carried horizontal siding. The discovery was corroborated when a substance found on the outside of the chord was identified as lead paint.

Architectural elevation drawings and measurements, old photographs, and a copy of Lemuel Chenoweth's plans for the bridge were provided by Turner's commissioners.

A painting by Mrs. M.D. Pool of Virginia, probably done sometime in the mid-1800s, provided the only graphic documentation of the bridge with exposed arches.

Turner used these resources and her own research to arrive at the final painting which includes: horizontal off-white siding, exposed arches and chords, brick-red wooden roof shingles, wall studs, wooden curbs, hub rails, arched portals, gable end siding aligned with top chord, knee braces from truss posts to tie beams, bracing at center long posts on pier and abutments, restored pier and abutment stonework and a 10-inch camber, or rise, in the center of the span, which had dropped over the years. The drawing for the painting is measured and done to a scale of .1":4.58." Ten months were required to complete the project.

The original painting is a water color on 300 lb. paper with an image of 17" x 28". It has been reproduced by offset lithography, in a limited edition of 300 signed and numbered prints plus two artists, proofs, on 100 lb. acid-free paper. It's image size is 26" x 15-3/4". For more information contact, Laurelwood Studio, Rt. 2 Box J, Jane Lew, WV 26378

About the Photographer

Stephen J. Shaluta Jr. is a native of north central West Virginia who now lives in Charleston, with his daughter Amy.

Steve began taking pictures around his home town of Grafton in 1978. Seven years later he resigned his job of 14 years as a locomotive engineer to pursue his dream career of photography.

His current position, as a photographer, with the West Virginia Division of Tourism and Parks, a job he has held since December 1985, allows him to spend time in the outdoor settings he loves. He considers it a dream job photographing the state's ski resorts, whitewater rafting rivers, various tourist attractions, and breathtaking natural beauty.

He does all his black and white darkroom work and E-6 color slide processing. He has experience assembling and presenting audio/visual slide programs, and gives photography workshops and seminars throughout the Mid-Atlantic region.

Steve, Arnout Hyde Jr. and Gerald Ratliff have combined their photographic talents in their recently finished book, *New River...A Photographic Essay*, which became available in June 1991.

Some of Steve's more recent publication credits include...*Outdoor Photographer, Southern Living, Time, Mid-Atlantic Country, Inc., Blue Ridge Country, West Virginia It's You!, Wonderful West Virginia* and more. To date Steve has 51 magazine front cover and seven calendar front cover credits.

Bibliography

Auvil, Myrtle, *Covered Bridges of West Virginia*, Third Edition, McClain Printing Co., Parsons, 1977.

Carnes, Eva Margaret, *Centennial History of the Philippi Covered Bridge 1852-1952*, Barbour County Historical Society, Inc., Philippi, 1952.

Harner, Harvey W., *Covered Bridges of Harrison County, West Virginia*, Education Foundation, Charleston, 1956.

Kemp, Emory L., *West Virginia's Historic Bridges*, West Virginia Department of Culture and History, West Virginia Department of Highways, Federal Highway Administration, 1984.